101 BRAIN PUZZLERS

101 BRAIN PUZZLERS

E.R. EMMET

BELL PUBLISHING COMPANY
New York

To Richard and Brian and the many others
on whom these were tried out

This 1982 edition is published by Bell Publishing Company,
distributed by Crown Publishers, Inc., by arrangement with
Emerson Books, Inc.

Previously published as *Brain Puzzler's Delight*

Manufactured in the United States of America

Library of Congress Cataloging in Publication Data

Emmet, E. R. (Eric Revell)
101 brain puzzles.

Originally published as: 101 brain-puzzlers
for the young of all ages. London: Macmillan,
1967.
Reprint. Originally published: Brain
puzzler's delight. 8th printing. Buchanan,
N.Y.: Emerson Books, 1978, c1970.
1. Mathematical recreations. 2. Puzzles.
I. Title. II. Title: One hundred one brain
puzzles. III. Title: One hundred and one
brain puzzles.
QA95.E4 1982 793.7'4 82-4379
AACR2

ISBN: 0-517-385597

h g f e d c b a

Contents

Preface

The making up of puzzles has become for me over the years a sort of compulsive habit. Some of the problems in this book obviously date, but most of them have been made up during the last year. I am grateful to the *Sunday Times* for permission to reprint Nos. 81 and 83, which appeared in their 'Brain-Teasers'. None of the others have previously appeared in print.

People differ considerably in their attitude to and aptitude for problems of this kind. Some find them an engaging challenge, for others the mind automatically switches off. I believe that most people can get pleasure and satisfaction from such intellectual exercises if they can learn to tackle them with some degree of confidence. The puzzles in this book are of very varying difficulty, and I hope that many readers may be encouraged, by a satisfactory solution of some of the easier ones, to tackle the more complicated activities of 'Our Factory'. In no case is any mathematical knowledge required beyond the most elementary. The fully worked out solutions are of course designed to help and encourage those who have little experience of this kind of thinking.

Different readers will be interested in different kinds of problems. I have tried to make each one independent, so that neither the question nor the solution depends in any significant way on anything that has gone before.

I am grateful to a large number of people, mostly members of my mathematical sets at Winchester, on whom the problems have been tried out. But most especially I owe a great debt of gratitude to Richard Longmore and Brian Orange who have each checked all the problems and solutions in detail, have discovered a number of errors, and have made a great many most helpful suggestions for clarification. I need hardly say that any errors which may still remain are entirely my responsibility.

The production of the typescript for a book like this is

inevitably complicated and difficult, and I am most grateful to Mrs. J. H. Preston and Miss P. Kerswell for the skill and patience with which they have done this job.

E. R. EMMET

PART ONE

Miscellaneous — Easy

1—13

1. Wedding Predictions

George, John, Arthur and David are married, but not necessarily respectively, to Christine, Eve, Prudence and Rose. They remember that at a party years ago various predictions had been made. George had said that John would not marry Christine. John had said that Arthur would marry Prudence. Arthur had predicted that whoever David married it would not be Eve. David, who at that time was more interested in football than in matrimony, had predicted that Arsenal would win the F.A. Cup next year. The only one to predict correctly was the man who later married Prudence.

Who married whom? Did Arsenal win the F.A. Cup the next year?

2. The Engine-driver's Shirt

Jones, Brown, Smith and Robinson were, not necessarily respectively, an Engine-driver, a Stoker, a Guard and a Porter. They wore, again not necessarily respectively, red, blue, black and green shirts.

You are told that the Engine-driver beat Brown at billiards and that Smith and the Guard often played golf with the men in black and green shirts. Jones and the Porter both disliked the man in the green shirt, but this was not the Stoker as he always wore a red shirt.

What was the colour of the Engine-driver's shirt? And what was the occupation and colour of the shirt of each of them?

3. Who Killed Popoff?

Algernon, Bertie and Clarence had so often expressed their opinion about Professor Popoff that when he was found murdered (stabbed to death with a dagger, but in a thoroughly gentlemanly way) it was natural that they should be suspected. In fact, for reasons into which we need not now go, it may be taken as certain that one of them is guilty. They made statements as follows:

ALGERNON: 1. I hadn't seen Popoff or had any contact with him for a week before his unfortunate demise.
2. Everything that Bertie says is true.
3. Everything that Clarence says is true.

BERTIE: 1. I have never handled a dagger.
2. Everything that Algernon says is false.
3. Everything that Clarence says is false.

CLARENCE: 1. Algernon was talking to Popoff just before he was killed.
2. Bertie has handled a dagger.
3. I have for a long time thought more of Popoff than is generally realised.

Looking back on the tragic event now, it is interesting to see that Algernon and Bertie both made the same number of true statements. (This number can be anything from 0 to 3).

Who killed Popoff?

4. Rithmetic Road

Alf, Bert and Duggie all live in different houses in Rithmetic Road.

By a curious coincidence, the age of each man is either seven greater or seven less than the number of his house. All of them are over 15 years old and less than 90; their ages are all different.

Alf said that the number of Bert's house was even, and Bert remarked that the number of his house was greater than that of Duggie's. 'My age,' he added proudly, 'is a perfect cube.'

Charlie said that the number of his house was greater by 3 than that of Alf's, and that Duggie's age was an exact multiple of Alf's age.

Duggie, who has an unfortunate habit of complicating things, said that Bert's age was either 27 or an even number other than 64. 'Furthermore,' he commented, 'Charlie does not live at number 19.'

These remarks were unfortunately not all true. It was interesting to note that all remarks made by anyone who lived in an even-numbered house were false, and all remarks made by anyone who lived in an odd-numbered house were true.

What are their ages and the numbers of their houses?

5. The Cricket Dinner

The M.C.C. (Mathematicians' Cricket Club), to which I belong, always holds its annual dinner in January. I was trying to find the date of the next dinner from some fellow members, but they were being rather foolishly unhelpful. One of them told me that the date was an odd number, another that it was greater than 13. A third told me that it was not a perfect square and a fourth that it was a perfect cube. And finally Charles Computer, the captain of the club, told me that the date was less than my highest score last season. (This was in fact 17, and I thought it was rather nice of Computer to bring this in.)

I subsequently discovered that of all these five statements only one was true.

What was the date of the dinner?

6. On the Tiles

A rectangular floor is composed of square tiles of the same size, 81 along one side, 63 along the other.

If a straight line is drawn diagonally across the floor from corner to corner how many tiles will it cross?

What would the answer be if there were 472 tiles along one side and 296 along the other?

7. Homes, Houses and Hopes

Adolphus, Basil, Cyril and Desmond, when young, hoped to become an Author, a Brewer, a Card-sharper and a Doctor. They were members of A, B, C and D houses in the same school, and they came from Australia, Brazil, Cheltenham and Dalmatia. The letter of each man's house and the initial letters of his youthful ambition, his home and his name are all different from each other. The would-be Doctor had never been to Brazil, and the would-be Brewer had never been to Cheltenham.

When they were young Cyril, the boy from Australia and the would-be Brewer all used to spend their holidays together.

What was the ambition, the home and the house of each of them?

8. Vests and Vocations

Mr Baker, Mr Carpenter, Mr Hunter and Mr Walker were not respectively, a baker, a carpenter, a hunter and a walker by profession. They were in the habit of wearing, again not respectively, a brown, a cerise, a heliotrope and a white shirt. No man's profession was the same as his name and the colour of each man's shirt began with a letter which was different from the initial letter both of his name and of his profession.

Mr Hunter and the professional walker dined together regularly. The hunter, rather curiously, violently disliked the colour brown and would never wear a brown shirt. Mr Carpenter was the baker.

Find the profession of each man and the colour of his shirt.

9. Ping Pong Pill Passes On

The eminent Chinese professor, Ping Pong Pill, was found murdered in the waiting room at Bingchester Station. He was seen alive by several people at 9.25½, and his mangled corpse was discovered at 9.28½.

Bingchester is an important junction where lines cross thus:

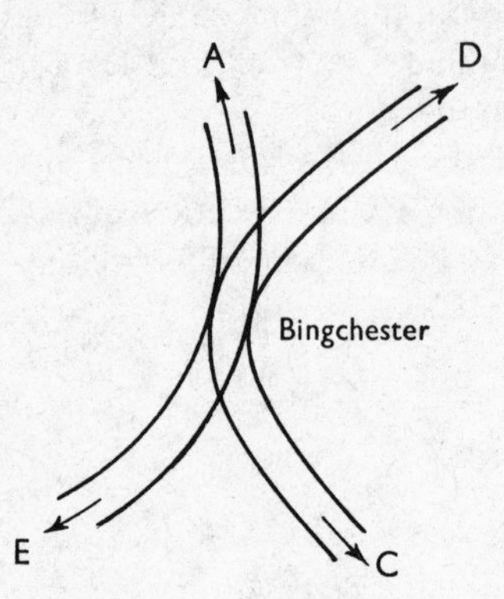

A, C, D, E represent stations on the lines.

An extract from the time-table reads thus:

A	9.15	C	9.10	D	8.55	E	8.58
B arr.	9.23	B arr.	9.27	B arr.	9.26	B arr.	9.22
dep.	9.25	dep.	9.30	dep.	9.29	dep.	9.25
C	9.44	A	9.38	E	9.53	D	9.56

In each case the trains run every quarter of an hour, so that the times of the trains before or after can be discovered by subtracting or adding 15 minutes.

The railway system has recently been nationalised; all trains therefore are now precisely punctual.

There are five persons suspected of the murder, and it may be taken as *certain* that one of them is guilty. They all have bicycles, and when cycling they move at a steady average speed of 15 m.p.h.

The distances of A, C, D, E from Bingchester by road are:
A 4 miles, C 7 miles, D 10 miles, E 7 miles.

The areas between A, C, D, E are covered by sea, impenetrable swamps, impassable mountains and notices saying 'Private: No Entrance'. It is therefore not possible for anyone to get from one of these places to another without passing through Bingchester either by road or by train.

The five gentlemen who are suspected make statements, which are all true, as follows:

SMITH: I saw Jones in A at 9.14 and I was in E at 9.52.

BROWN: I was in E at 9.1, and in C at 9.58.

JONES: I was in D at 10.9. I left my bicycle at A.

ROBINSON: I was in C at 8.56, and in D at 10.3.

GREEN: I was in A at 9.40, and in E at 8.59.

They can of course take their bicycles on the train, but no one uses anybody else's bicycle. Two bicycles were found at Bingchester.

Whose were they? What were the exact movements of all five of them?

Who killed Ping Pong Pill?

10. Liars Again

Smith, Jones and Robinson each make four statements as follows:

SMITH:
1. Jones owes me £1.
2. Robinson owes me 5*s*.
3. All Robinson's statements are true.
4. All Jones's statements are untrue.

JONES:
1. I owe no money to Smith.
2. Robinson owes me 10*s*.
3. I'm British.
4. All Smith's statements are untrue.

ROBINSON:
1. I owe no money to anybody.
2. Jones is a Dutchman.
3. I always tell the truth.
4. Two of Jones's statements are true and two are false.

One person made 4 true statements.

Who? Find, for all of them, which statements are true and which false.

11. The Poison Spreads

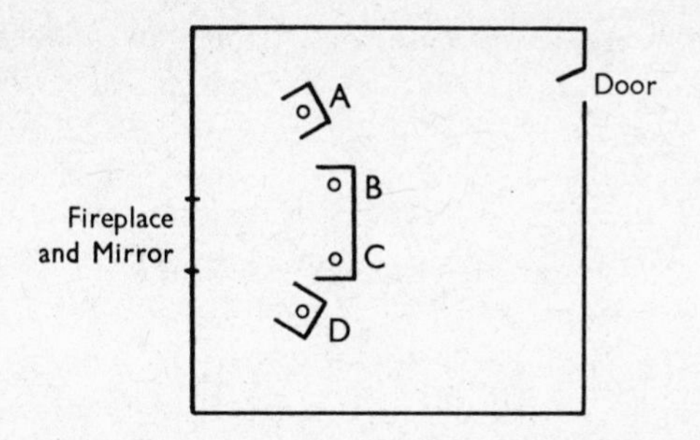

Bilks the bookmaker has just been found dead in the dining-room of the club. Poison in his wine.

Four men seated as above on a sofa and two armchairs round the fireplace in the lounge are discussing the murder. Their names are Smith, Brown, Jones and Robinson. They are, not necessarily respectively, a General, a Schoolmaster, an Admiral and a Doctor.

i. The waiter has just poured out a glass of whisky for Jones and of beer for Brown.
ii. The General looks up and in the mirror over the fireplace sees the door close behind the waiter. He then turns to Robinson, who is next to him, and starts talking.
iii. Neither Smith nor Brown have got any sisters.
iv. The Schoolmaster is a teetotaller.
v. Smith, who is sitting in one of the armchairs, is the Admiral's brother-in-law. The Schoolmaster is next to him on his left.
vi. Suddenly a hand is seen stealthily putting something in Jones's whisky. It is the murderer again. No one has left his seat; nobody else is in the room.

Who is the murderer?
What is the profession of each man, and where is he sitting?

12. The Mathematics Paper

Alf, Bert, Charlie, Duggie and Ernie have been doing a mathematics paper consisting of 5 questions. If the answer was right 10 marks were given, if the answer was wrong either 7, 2, or 0 marks were given according to the method used and the way in which the work was set out. (No mark other than 10, 7, 2 or 0 was awarded for any question. *It is perfectly possible for two people to get the same wrong answer, but be given different marks*)

At least one person got each question right. Some information about the answers which different people got and the totals of the marks obtained by different people and for different questions is shown below. You may also find it helpful to know that Ernie got more marks for question 5 than Bert did.

No. of question	1	2	3	4	5	Total of marks
Alf	5′		11		4·5	34
Bert	3′ 6″	17	5		3·4	19
Charlie	4′	43	5		2·8	31
Duggie	2′ 6″	17	11	6*s*.	3·8	
Ernie	7′	17	7	7*s*.	5·2	9
Totals of marks for different questions	14	29	22	42		

Find the correct answers to all the questions and the number of marks obtained by each person for each question.

13. Abacus Avenue

A, B, C, D, E live in Abacus Avenue which, rather curiously. has houses numbered from 10 to 111 inclusive. Two of them live in the same house, the other three in different houses.

They make various remarks, not all true, about their houses.

A: 1. My number is a factor of B's.
   2. E's number is 10 greater than D's.

B: 1. My number is over 70.
   2. A's number is more than 30.

C: 1. My number is a cube and a square.
   2. D's number is greater than 50.

D: 1. My number is a square.
   2. B's number is a cube.

E: 1. My number is twice B's.

A study of these remarks revealed the rather curious fact that all the statements made by those who lived in houses whose numbers were greater than 50 were false; all statements made by the others were true.

Find the numbers of all their houses.

PART TWO

Football Matches

14—24

14.

A, B and C all play each other once at football.

Table of results (not necessarily in order of points scored), with some of the figures missing, is as follows:

	Played	Won	Lost	Drawn	Goals for	Goals against
A	2	1			4	
B	2				3	0
C	2			1	2	

Find the score in each match.

15.

A, B, C and D all play each other once at football. Some of the figures in the table of results (in which they are not necessarily arranged in the order of points scored) are given below.

	Played	Won	Lost	Drawn	Goals for	Goals against
A	3					5
B	3	3			4	
C	3					
D	3			1	0	3

With the additional information that the match between A and C was a draw (3–3) and that A scored more than 5 goals altogether, you should be able to *fill up the gaps in the table and find the score in each match.*

16.

A, B, C, D are all to play each other once at football. Some of the figures in the table after *some* of the matches have been played are given below.

	Played	*Won*	*Lost*	*Drawn*	*Goals for*	*Goals against*
A	2	1			3	3
B	2			1	4	
C	2					
D				1	4	7

You are told that A beat B by 3–1.

Find who played whom and the score in each match.

17.

Three teams A, B, C played each other at football, and the results of their games were set out in the usual form. Unfortunately ink was spilt on my copy, and all that I was able to read was as follows:

	Played	*Won*	*Lost*	*Drawn*	*Goals for*	*Goals against*
A	2	2				
B	2					
C	2			1	3	

I was showing this to my friend, Kickham, who is a member of the A team and also an intelligent person. He knew the complete details of all the games. After a little thought, he said, 'It's interesting that the facts happen to be such that if you knew the total number of goals scored by A you would be able to fill up the table and find the score in every match.'

Fill up the table and find the score in each match.

18.

A, B, C, D, E are all to play each other once at football. The following table gives a certain amount of information about the situation when *some* of the matches have been played. (Two points are given for a win and one for a draw.)

	Played	*Won*	*Lost*	*Drawn*	*Goals for*	*Goals against*	*Points*
A	4			0	3	1	
B	3				4	4	
C	4			2			
D				2	3	2	4
E					4	5	1

C scored 3 goals against B.

Find who played whom and the score in each match. (The teams are not necessarily arranged in the order of points scored.)

19.

Five teams A, B, C, D, E are all to play each other once at football.

The following table, in which the order is not necessarily one of merit, gives some information about the situation when *some* of the matches have been played. (Two points are given for a win and one for a draw.)

	Played	*Won*	*Lost*	*Drawn*	*Goals for*	*Goals against*	*Points*
A	4				7	1	5
B					5	2	
C	3		0			4	3
D	4				5		3
E	2				2	6	0

Find who has played whom and the score in each match.

20.

A, B, C, D, E are five teams which are all to play each other once at football. The following table (in which the teams are not necessarily arranged in the order of points scored) gives some information about the situation after *most* of the matches have been played. (Two points are given for a win and one for a draw.)

	Played	*Won*	*Lost*	*Drawn*	*Goals for*	*Goals against*	*Points*
A	4				8	1	5
B	3				7	2	
C	3	0				5	3
D	2						1
E	2				0	5	0

Find who played whom, and the score in each match.

21.

Five football teams — A, B; C, D, E — all play each other once. The order of merit giving numbers of matches won, lost, drawn, the goals for and against, and the points scored (2 points for a win, 1 for a draw) is seen below, but unfortunately owing to the clumsy spilling of some ink, a good many figures were illegible and are left blank.

	Played	*Won*	*Lost*	*Drawn*	*Goals for*	*Goals against*	*Points*
C	4		1		7		6
A	4					7	
E	4			1	9		5
B	4			3		3	
D	4					3	1

(If teams are equal on points in this order of merit, the one with the superior goal average is put higher.) With the additional information that A scored 4 goals against C, but did not score as many as 4 in any other match, and that E scored 5 goals against A and 2 against B, you should be able to *find the score in each match.*

22. Blots on the Evidence

Four school houses, A, B, C, D played each other at football. I found my friend Alf who is a member of the A house team looking with some interest at a very messy piece of paper which he had just picked up on which all that could be read was as follows:

	Played	*Won*	*Lost*	*Drawn*	*Goals for*	*Goals against*
A						
B		3			5	2
C	3			1	4	8
D	3					1

Alf, of course, knew the scores in all the matches in which A House played, but before seeing this piece of paper he knew nothing about the scores or results in the other matches. After a bit of reflection, however, he said 'I can now tell you the score in every match that was played'. (He does so, and he is quite right).

It would be asking too much to expect you to do the same with the information available. But if I also give you some information that Alf did not have, namely that at least one goal was scored in every match, that the score between D and A was the same as the score between B and C (in that order), you too should be able to *discover the same in every match.*

23. Muddle and Mess Once More

A, B, C, D, E are all to play each other once at football. After *some* of the matches have been played a table is produced giving some information about numbers of matches played, numbers won, lost, drawn, goals for and against and points scored. (Two points are given for a win and one for a draw.) Unfortunately, however, some mistakes were made and many of the figures were illegible.

All that could be read was:

	Played	*Won*	*Lost*	*Drawn*	*Goals for*	*Goals against*	*Points*
A	3				1		3
B	3				2	3	4
C	3			2		1	3
D	3			0			2
E	3				3	4	1

Of these figures *two* are wrong. Nevertheless if I give you the information that B played C, you should be able to *discover which of the figures are wrong, and also who played whom and the score in each match.*

24. Uncle Claudius Again

Uncle Claudius has been making up puzzles again. His latest was about the results of football matches in which four teams A, B, C, D all play each other once. Unfortunately in setting out the table he made various mistakes and also spilt some ink. All that could be read was as follows. (Two points are given for a win and one for a draw.)

	Played	*Won*	*Lost*	*Drawn*	*Goals for*	*Goals against*	*Points*
A	3				7	1	5
B	3				5	3	
C	3			2	4	4	
D	3				0	9	0

Fortunately of the figures left only one is wrong. If I also tell you that C scored 2 goals against B you should be able to discover which figure is wrong, to *fill up the table correctly and find the exact score in each match.* (The four teams are not necessarily placed in descending order of points scored.)

PART THREE

Missing Digits (Decimal Scale)

25—39

25. Hitler and Goering

Below is an addition sum with letters substituted for digits. The same letter stands for the same digit wherever it appears, and different letters stand for different digits.

```
    H I T L E R
  G O E R I N G
  -------------
  H T T L L H H H
  -------------
```

Find the digits for which the letters stand.

26.

Fill in the missing digits, including the figures in the quotient, in the following division sum:

```
         ___________________
- - - ) - - - - - 5 - - - 8
        - - -
        -----
          - - - -
            - - -
          -------
                - - - -
                - - - -
                -------
                    - - - -
                    - - - -
                    -------

                    -------
```

27.

Find the missing digits, and the quotient.

```
          _________________
- - - )  - - - - - o -
           - - 5
           -----
             - - -
             - - -
           -------
             - - - -
               - - -
         -----------
                 - - - -
                 - - - -
                 -------

                 -------
```

28.

Find the missing digits and the quotient in the following division sum

```
        ____________
- - )  - -
       - -
       ---
       - - -
       - - -
       -----
         - - -
         - - -
         -----
             - -
             - -
             ---

             ---
```

29.

A division sum. *Find the missing digits.* (The two *a*s stand for the same digit, but there is no implication that this digit does not occur elsewhere).

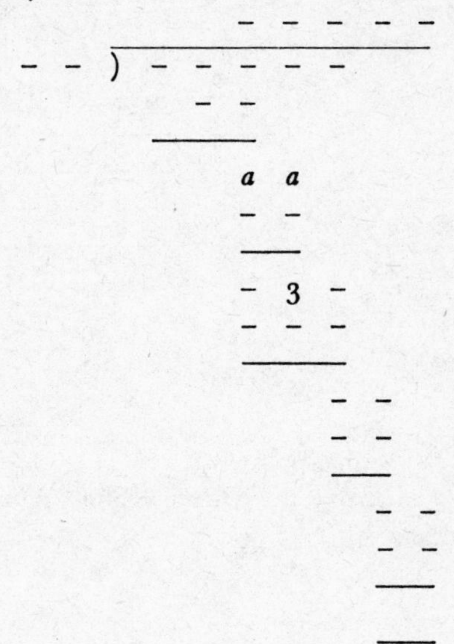

30.

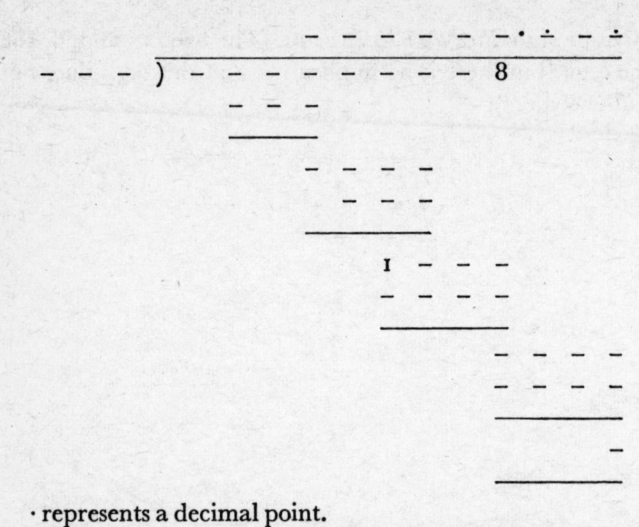

· represents a decimal point.

∸ – ∸ indicates that these three decimal figures recur.

Find the missing digits.

31.

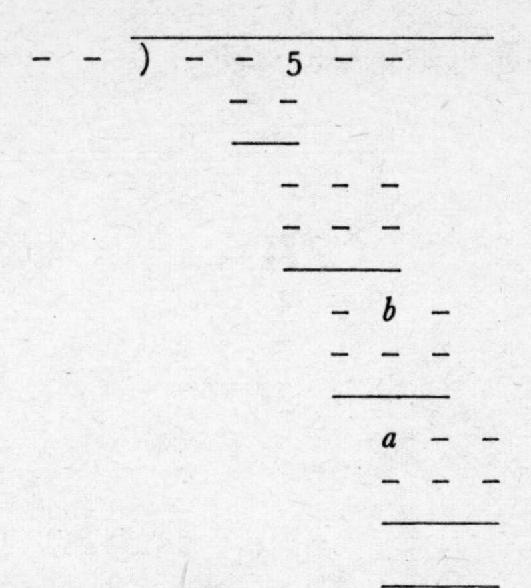

A division sum. *Find the missing digits and the quotient.*

a, b, stand for digits which are such that $a - b = 2$. (These are not necessarily the only places where these digits occur.)

32.

A division sum. *Find the missing digits*:

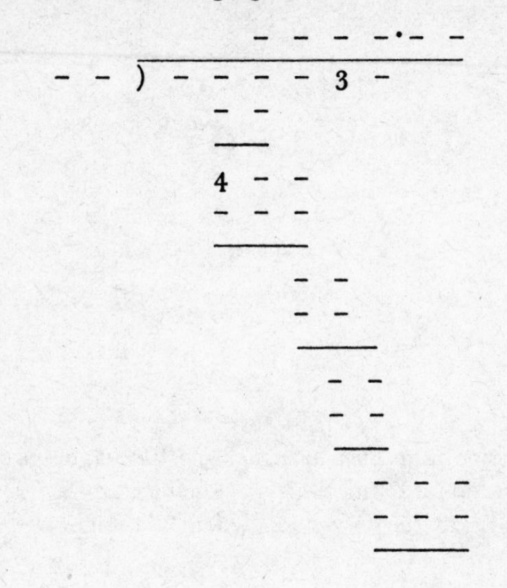

33.

A division sum. *Find the missing digits.* (*a* stands for the same digit wherever it occurs. But it does not necessarily follow that this digit does not occur elsewhere.)

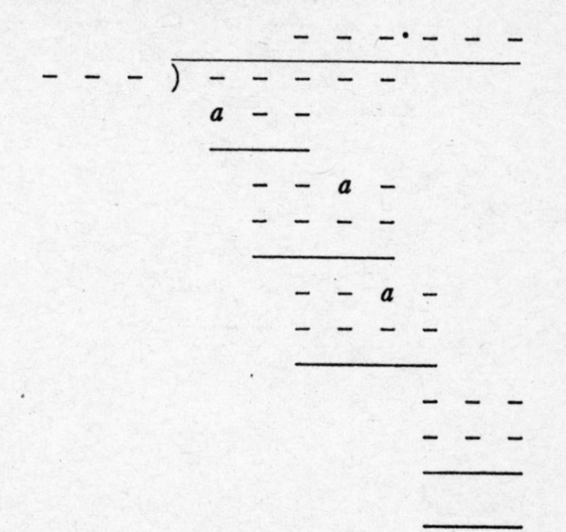

34.

Find the missing digits in the following division sum.
(· represents a decimal point; the division comes out exactly.)

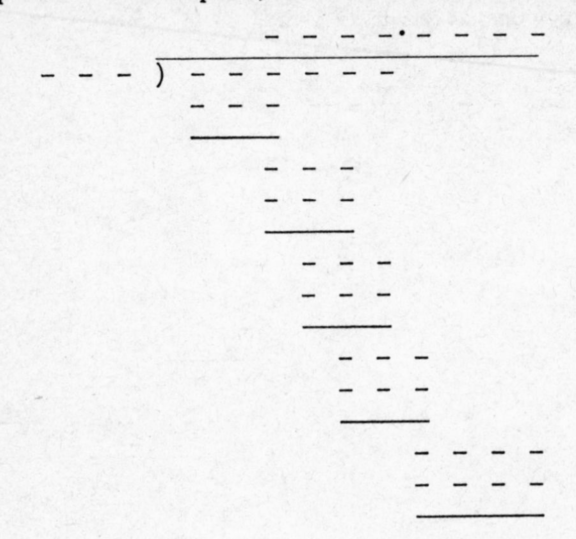

35.

```
(i)  - - c        (ii)  - - -
       - b                - -
     -----              -----
       - a              - - a
     -----              -----
```

(i) and (ii) represent the same two numbers being in one case added together, in the other case subtracted. There are no 0s appearing anywhere. The digits represented by the two *a*s are the same. $b - c = 1$.

In neither (i) nor (ii) does the same digit appear more than once.

Find all the digits.

36.

```
              -·- -
       ----------
 - - ) - - -
       - -
       -----
         - -
         - -
         ---
           - -
           - -
           ---

           ---
```

There are two alternative solutions to the above division.

Find them both.

37.

```
(i)      - - -        (ii)  - - -
           - -                a b
     ---------             -------
     - - - -                b - a
     ---------             -------
```

(i) and (ii) represent the same two numbers being in one case added together, in the other case subtracted. In (i) all the digits are different; in (ii) there are two pairs of digits which are the same, represented by the two *a*s and the two *b*s, but otherwise the digits are all different. The digits in the result of the addition are all different from any of the digits in the result of the subtraction.

Find the missing digits.

38.

A division sum:

```
             a  -  -  -  -  -  -·-  -
         ----------------------------
 -  -  )  -  -  -  -  d  -  -  -  a
             -  -
          ------
             b  c  -
             -  -  -
             -------
                   -  -
                   -  -
                   ----
                      a  -  -
                      -  -  -
                      -------
                            -  -
                            -  -
                            ----
                               -  -
                               -  -
                               ----
                                  -  -  -
                                  -  -  -
                                  -------

                                  -------
```

The three *a*s stand for the same digit. $b-c=2$; *a*, *b*, *c* and *d* are all different digits. (The places indicated are not necessarily the only places where *a*, *b*, *c* and *d* occur.)

Find the missing digits.

39.

Addition and division:

```
                                        - - - - -
                                ___________________
(i)   - - - -       (ii) - - )  - - - - o o
          - -                   - -
     _________                  ___
     - - - - -                    - - -
     _________                      - -
                                  _______
                                      - - -
                                      - - -
                                      _____
                                          -
                                      _____
```

(i) shows a 4-figure number and a 2-figure number added together.

(ii) shows the same 4-figure number multiplied by 100, divided by the same 2-figure number. (It will be seen that the division leaves a remainder.)

Find the missing digits.

PART FOUR

Missing Digits (Binary and Other Scales)

40—43

40.

A multiplication in binary.

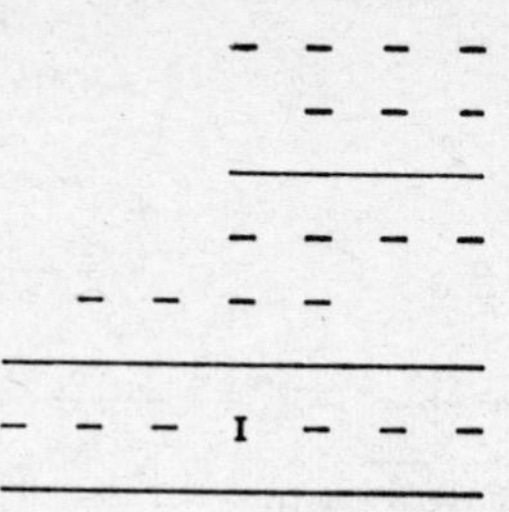

Find the missing digits.

41.

The following division is in binary arithmetic.

```
              _ _ _ _
          ___________
_ _ _ _ ) _ _ _ _ _ _ 1
          _ _ _ _
          _______
              _ _ _ _
              _ _ _ _
              _______
                _ _ _ _
                _ _ _ _
                _______

                _______
```

Find the missing digits.

42.

Three different scales:

```
(a)   –     (b)       –     (c)          –
      –             – –                – –
      –             – –              – – –
   ______        ________        __________
      –           – – –            – – – –
   ______        ________        __________
```

a, *b*, *c* represent the same three numbers being added together on three different scales. In no case is the scale greater than ten.

Find the scale of each set of numbers and find all the missing digits.

43.

(i) – – (on the decimal scale) = (ii) – – – – – – (on the scale of ?)
= (iii) – – (on the scale of 6) = (iv) – – multiplied by – – – – – (in prime factors, both on the same scale)

Find all the missing digits.

PART FIVE

Miscellaneous — Not So Easy

44—56

44. The Christmas Party

If only the Joneses had been there, as expected, we would have been just right for some fours at bridge. And if only those horrible Higginbottles hadn't turned up — no one had invited them — we could have played 'Strip the Pillow' (an old Scottish game for which the players have to be divided into 5 equal groups of not less than 4 each). I thought at one time the room was going to burst, though it wasn't as bad as that awful day when we had 30 people in it.

The numbers of Joneses and Higginbottles are different. There are less than 5 of each.

How many people were there at the party?

45. Alf, Bert and Charlie in the Classroom

Alf, Bert, Charlie, Duggie and Ernie are members, not necessarily respectively, of A, B, C, D, E houses at their school, and the five of them have just been placed in an order of merit (no ties) in the competition for the Hebrew Verse prize for which they were the only entrants.

They make remarks about their houses and their places in the competition as follows:

ALF: (i) Charlie was lower than Bert.
(ii) Duggie is in D House.

BERT: (i) Ernie was lower than Charlie.
(ii) Duggie is in C House.

CHARLIE: (i) Alf is in C House.
(ii) The man in B house was not second.

DUGGIE: (i) Charlie is in E House.
(ii) Ernie is not in D House.

ERNIE: (i) I was lower than Bert.
(ii) Alf was first.

It is interesting to note that remarks in which the first person mentioned was lower in the order of merit than the speaker are true, and remarks in which the first person mentioned was higher than the speaker are false. When making remarks about themselves only those who were first or second in the order of merit tell the truth.

Find the order of merit and each person's house.

46. The Christmas Compensation Club

Gerald, Harold, Ian, John and Karl have long been keen members of the Christmas Compensation Club — open only to those who suffer the severe loss which results from having one's birthday on Christmas day, and have not yet reached the age of 90.

Last Christmas Karl was older than Ian by three times as much as he was older than Harold, and John was 10 per cent younger than Harold and 20 per cent older than Ian. The difference between the ages of Gerald and Karl is the same as the difference between the ages of John and Ian (and in the same sense).

Find their ages.

47. The Years Roll By

Arthur, Bill, Colin, Donald and Eric, having nothing better to do, are making remarks about their own and each others ages — as follows:

ARTHUR: Eric is 27.

BILL: I'm 81.

COLIN: Bill is 61.

DONALD: (i) Arthur is 57.
(ii) What Colin says is false.

ERIC: (i) Bill is older than Arthur.
(ii) Donald is 30 years younger than Colin.

(None of them is less than 10 or more than 99).

Remarks made by anyone who is 50 or over are true, unless his age is a perfect square. Remarks made by anyone who is under 50 are false, unless his age is a perfect cube.

Find all their ages.

48. Sinister Street

Agnes and Beatrice live in different dwellings in Sinister Street, which has houses numbered from 1 to 99. Neither of them knows the number of the other's house. Xerxes lives in the same street — in a different house of course — and the ladies are anxious to know where.

Agnes asks Xerxes two questions:

1. Is your number a perfect square?
2. Is it greater than 50?

Having heard the answers she claims that she knows Xerxes' number and writes it down. But she is wrong, which is not surprising considering that only the second of Xerxes' answers is true.

Beatrice, who has heard none of this, then asks Xerxes two different questions:

1. Is your number a perfect cube?
2. Is it greater than 25?

And like Agnes, when she has heard the answers, she claims to know where Xerxes lives. But again, like Agnes, she is wrong, for Xerxes has only answered the second question truthfully.

If I give you the additional information that Xerxes' number is less than that of Agnes or Beatrice, and that the sum of their three numbers is a perfect square multiplied by two, you should be able to *discover where they all three live.*

49. Youthful Ambitions

Arthur, Basil, Clarence, Dudley and Ethelred are married, but not respectively, to Alice, Barbara, Clarissa, Dorothy and Eve. The birthplaces of the five men were, not respectively, Andover, Bristol, Chippenham, Delhi and Ealing; and, a most intimate and revealing detail, their youthful ambitions were, again not respectively, to have become an Anarchist, a Barber, A Cheese-Parer, a Dog-fancier and an Entomologist.

For each man his name, the name of his wife, his home town and his youthful ambition all begin with different letters.

The five ladies make remarks (which are unfortunately not all true) as follows:

ALICE: The would-be Dog-fancier is married to Barbara.

BARBARA: 1. The man who wanted to become an Entomologist is not Dorothy's husband.

2. The man who was born in Bristol has always wanted to be a Dog-fancier.

CLARISSA: The man who was born in Andover is married to Barbara.

DOROTHY: The would-be Barber is not my husband.

EVE: 1. The man who was born in Andover is not Basil.

2. The man who was born in Chippenham wanted to become an Entomologist.

It is interesting to notice that, in these remarks, when the subject of the sentence is a man whose name begins with a letter which comes before the initial letter of the speaker in the alphabet, the sentence is *true*; if the initial letter of the subject's name comes after the initial letter of the speaker's name, the sentence is false. In no case is the initial letter of the subject's name the same as the initial letter of the speaker's name.

Find, for each man, the name of his wife, his home town and his youthful ambition.

50. Alpha Avenue

Penelope lives in Alpha Avenue (which has houses numbered from 3 to 99 inclusive), and Quintin, her admirer, is anxious to know the number of her house.

Alf, Bert, Charlie and Duggie all have a certain amount of information about this number.

Alf	knows whether		it's a perfect square.
Bert	,,	,,	,, ,, multiple of 3.
Charlie	,,	,,	it has one figure or two.
Duggie	,,	,,	it's a multiple of 5.

After asking Alf, Bert and Charlie about their knowledge, Quintin thinks that he might attain certainty about the number if he can persuade Duggie, who is reluctant to talk, to give his information too. Quintin eventually succeeds in getting Duggie to tell him whether it's a multiple of 5, and Quintin then says: 'If I knew whether the number was odd or even I would be able to tell you where she lives.'

He persuades Penelope to tell him whether her number is odd or even, and Quintin confidently calls that evening on where he now feels sure that she lives. He is disappointed, however, to find a house which has obviously been empty for some time.

This was a very unfortunate mistake, but it is not surprising in view of the fact that both Alf and Bert lied about whether the number was a perfect square and a multiple of 3. (The others told the truth).

Where does Penelope live?

51. Vestites Revealed

Algernon, Basil and Clarence are either English or Irish, either Conservative or Liberal, and either Vestite or Transvestite. In each case there is, as they all know, at least one of each.

They none of them know which the others are, but Algernon and Basil have both been told that if Clarence is an Irish Transvestite he cannot be a Liberal.

Basil asks Algernon whether he is a Conservative or a Liberal, and whether he is English or Irish. Algernon tells him.

After a pause for reflection Basil is able to announce correctly the full particulars (English or Irish, Vestite or Transvestite, Conservative or Liberal) of both Algernon and Clarence.

Find the full particulars for all three of them.

52. Uncle Knows Best

Uncle Claudius is a bit hard of hearing, so that when his nephew Bartholomew asked various neighbours who live in separate houses in Christmas Crescent some questions about the numbers of their houses he failed to hear the answers, though he heard the questions all right. Bartholomew has lived in Christmas Crescent for some time, and his uncle knows his number, but Claudius has only just bought a vacant house there and Bartholomew doesn't know about it.

The Crescent has houses numbered rather curiously from 5 to 105.

Bartholomew asked the same three questions to three people who live in separate houses in the Crescent — first to X, then Y, then Z.

(i) Is the number of your house a multiple of 4?
(ii) Is it a perfect square?
(iii) Is it a multiple of 9?

No two sets of three answers are the same in every respect.

After hearing X's answer Bartholomew says to him: 'If I knew whether the number of your house was greater than 83, I would know what it is.'

(Claudius hears his nephew say this and is able to write down X's number correctly.)

After hearing Y's answer Bartholomew says to him: 'If I knew whether your number was greater than 50 I could tell you what it is.'

(Claudius hears his nephew say this, and as he happens to know that Y's number is greater than his own, he is able to write it down correctly.)

After hearing Z's answer Bartholomew says to him: 'If I knew whether the number of your house was greater than 30 I could tell you what it is.'

(Claudius hears this and notes with interest that his own number is certainly less than Z's. But he too has no way of deciding whether Z's number is greater than 30. However he is anxious to keep the reputation he is building up for intelligence and intuition, guesses that it is greater than 30 and writes it down. Fortunately he is quite right.)

What are the numbers of the houses of Bartholomew, Claudius, X, Y and Z?

53. Acacia Avenue

A, B and C live in Acacia Avenue where the houses are numbered consecutively 2 to 65 (No. 1 was destroyed during the War.)

None of them know where the other two live, but they know that their numbers ascend in the order A, B, C. (In fact the difference between the numbers of any two of them is at least 4. But they don't know this.)

B asks C whether the number of his house is a perfect square. C answers. B thinks he's telling the truth. A, who overhears, thinks he's lying. A is right.

C asks A whether the number of his house is a perfect cube. A answers. B overhears.

A asks B whether the number of his house is a multiple of 23. B answers. C overhears.

After a pause for reflection and calculation A says that he knows where B lives and also knows that C must live in one of two houses; he writes down the answers. B says that he knows where A lives and writes down the answer. C says that he knows where both A and B live and writes down the answers. Every answer is wrong.

Where do A, B and C live?

54. The Willahs and the Wallahs

The inhabitants of a small island in the Pacific are divided into two tribes — the Willahs and the Wallahs. Every inhabitant has a different personal number; the numbers of the Willahs are all primes, and the numbers of the Wallahs are none of them primes.

Remarks made to people belonging to the same tribe as the speaker are always true; remarks made to someone belonging to a different tribe from the speaker are never true.

A, B, C, D, E, F are six natives, three belonging to each tribe. They make remarks as follows:

A to B: D is a Wallah.
B to D: F's number is half way between yours and C's.
C to E: I'm a Willah.
C to F: D's number is half way between yours and A's.
D to A: Our numbers are both less than 50.
E to A: I'm a Wallah.
E to B: My number is 35.
F to C: My number is greater than yours by ten.

Find to which tribe each person belongs and the numbers of as many of them as possible.

55. Out of the Window and Over the Wall

Alf, Bert and Charlie are in prison. It does not matter why. What is important is that they should get out as soon as possible,

Plan of possible exit

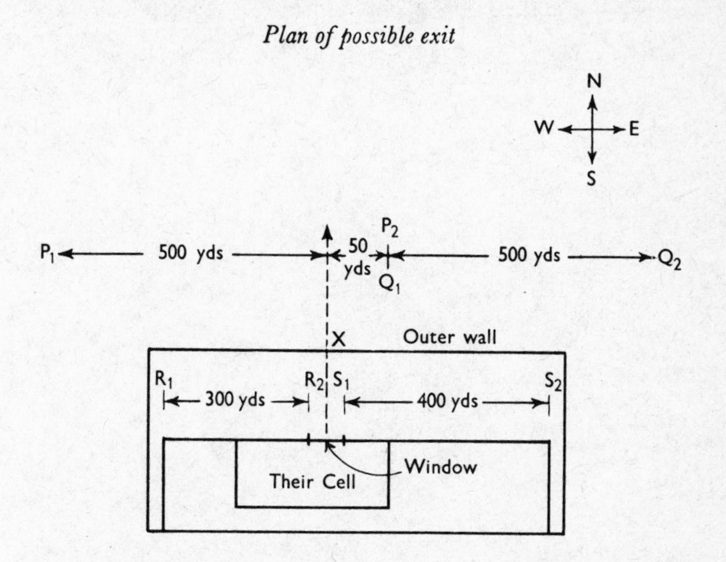

They have made arrangements for getting through the window of their cell, and over the outer wall at X. But they can only hope to escape unseen if they do it in the dark, one man at a time, and if each man has a clear two minutes with all the warder sentries at least 100 yards away.

They reckon that it is dark enough for their purposes at 9.0 p.m., and at that time a new lot of sentries come on duty. There are two sentries inside the outer wall. One starts at R_1, 300 yards west of a point outside their window, marches to R_2, exactly outside their window, and turns about. Another starts at S_1, outside their window, marches to S_2, 400 yards to the east, and turns about.

There are also two sentries outside the outer wall. One starts at P_1, 500 yards west of a point outside their window, marches 550 yards to P_2, 50 yards east of a point outside their window and turns about. The other sentry starts at Q_1 (the same point as P_2), marches 500 yards east to Q_2 and turns about.

The sentries start at 9 p.m. from the points P_1, Q_1, R_1, S_1 and march up and down their beats at a regular speed of 100 yards per minute. (Time spent in turning can be neglected.)

At what times should Alf, Bert and Charlie attempt to escape?

56. The World of Bonkers

In the World of Bonkers the ditty for remembering the numbers of days in their seven months runs as follows:

'Nineteen days hath Cucumber,
Strawberry too, and the number
of days there are in Tiddleywinks
is just the same as 'tis in Jinks,
which is seven whole days more
than the ten there are in Pinafore.
With the month of Collywobble
diary makers have some trouble;
thirteen days if year is even,
forty-four if odd. And Stephen
quite the least of Bonkers months,
in fact it's sometimes called the runt, as
you can easily understand,
since it hath but four days and
another two in years of Heaven
(that's if the year's date ends in seven).'

There are five days in each week—Joyday, Funday, Laughday, Blissday and Workday, in that order.

In the year 17 a.b. (after bliss) the King of Bonkers went off for his holiday on Funday, Strawberry 17th and returned, just over 7 weeks later, on Blissday, Tiddleywinks 8th.

In the year 19 a.b. there were exactly 10 weeks from Collywobble 41st to Pinafore 7th.

Collywobble is the first and most important month in the year.

1. *Find the order of the seven months of the Bonkers year.*

2. *In the year 21 a.b. Strawberry 13th was a Workday. What day of the week was Collywobble 2nd?*

PART SIX

Cross-Number Puzzles

57—64

57.

1		2	3	4
		5		
6	7		8	
9		10		
	11			

(There are no 0 s)

ACROSS

1. All digits are odd and all different.
5. Sum of digits is half the cube root of 3 down.
6. A prime number.
8. Three times the sum of its digits.
9. This number reversed is the square of an even number.
11. This is the same when reversed, and is divisible by 9.

DOWN

1. First three digits of 4 down rearranged.
2. A prime number.
3. A perfect cube.
4. Each digit is greater than the preceding one.
7. A multiple of 8 across.
10. The sum of the digits is the square of a perfect square.

58.

1	2	3	4	■
5				■
6		■	7	8
9		10		
	■	11		

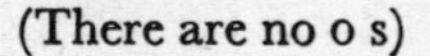

(There are no 0 s)

ACROSS

1. Square of 10 down.
5. Sum of digits is 12.
6. Odd, but not prime.
7. This number is larger when reversed; the sum of its digits is 7.
9. A perfect cube.
10. Square of product of two primes.
11. An odd number.

DOWN

1. A perfect cube.
2. An odd number; all digits different.
3. A prime.
4. Each digit is greater than preceding one.
8. A perfect square.
9. Factor of number formed by first three digits of 5 across.
10. A prime.

59.

(There are no 0 s)

ACROSS

1. An odd number, and a multiple of 9 across.
4. Multiple of cube root of 1 across.
5. The square of the product of two odd primes.
6. A perfect square. Less than 1 across.
7. A multiple of the sum of its digits.
9. Not a cube. Sum of digits is 9.
10. A prime number.
11. A prime number.
12. Odd. And odd when reversed. A prime number.

DOWN

1. The same when reversed.
2. Three of the digits are even and two odd. The sum of the even digits = the sum of the odd digits.
3. Each digit is less than the preceding one.
4. The cube of a cube.
8. A multiple of 11 across.
10. The sum of its digits = the sum of the digits of 10 across and also of 12 across.

60.

('There are no 0 s)

ACROSS

1. Multiple of 10 down.
5. Multiple of half 9 across.
6. A prime number.
7. Hold this up to a mirror and you will see a smaller number.
9. The difference between the first and second digits is the same as the difference between the second and third in that order.
11. The first digit divided by the second is equal to the second digit divided by the third.
12. The present age of a man whose age 8 years ago was the square of his son's age.

DOWN

2. A perfect square.
3. A multiple of a factor of the number formed by the first two digits of 5 across.
4. 1000 less than a perfect cube.
5. The second half is one greater than twice the first half.
8. This is greater than a perfect cube by 2.
9. Turn it upside down and it remains the same.
10. A multiple of a factor of 7 across.

(N.B. 7 across and 9 down are to be taken literally.)

61.

1	2	3	4	5
6			■	
■	7		8	■
9	10		11	12
13		14		

ACROSS

1. Product of two primes, each less than 1/3 of 4 across.
4. Multiple of sum of digits of 7 across.
6. Digits of 8 down re-arranged.
7. Multiple of 11 across.
9. A perfect cube.
11. When reversed this is 4 times a prime number.
13. Multiple of the sum of its digits.
14. A perfect cube.

DOWN

1. Multiple of half 5 down.
2. 4 times a prime number.
3. The same when reversed.
5. The square root of half 14 across.
8. A multiple of a factor of 11 across reversed.
9. A multiple of the square root of 8 down.
10. A prime number.
12. 8 times the sum of its digits.

62.

1	2	3	4	5
6			7	
		■	8	
■	9	10	11	
12			13	

(There are no 0 s)

ACROSS

1. Factor of first half of 9 across.
3. Multiple of 13 across.
6. The same when reversed; a perfect square.
7. A perfect square; a multiple of the sum of its digits.
8. A perfect cube.
9. Sum of digits = sum of digits of 5 down
12. Multiple of second half of 9 across.
13. A perfect square.

DOWN

1. Digits of 3 across in a different order.
2. An odd number. All digits are different. Number formed by first 3 digits is twice number formed by last 2.
3. Divisible by 11.
4. Divisible by 9.
5. Each digit greater than preceding one.
10. Multiple of 13 across.
11. The product of two of the digits of 5 down.

63.

1	2	3	4	
5				■
	■		6	7
8	9	10	11	
12		13		

ACROSS

1. Only two different digits are used in this odd number.
5. A perfect cube.
6. A prime number.
8. The same when reversed.
11. The first digit is the sum of the digits of 8 across.
12. A prime number multiplied by 2, and a prime number when reversed.
13. A perfect cube.

DOWN

1. The sum of the digits is a prime number which is greater than 19.
2. A prime number, and twice a prime number when reversed.
3. A multiple of the number formed by last two digits of 4 down.
4. Each digit is less than the preceding one.
7. A multiple of $\frac{1}{3}$ of 8 across.
9. A multiple of the cube root of 13 across.
10. 4 times the sum of its digits.

64. The Double Cross-Number

In this cross-number puzzle there are *two alternative sets of solutions* which fit the clues given. *You are asked to find them both.* In only two cases is the same square filled by the same digit in the two solutions. (There are no 0 s.)

ACROSS

1. A factor of number formed by second and third digits of 3 down.
3. Sum of digits is the same as the sum of the digits of 5 across.
5. The same when reversed. A perfect square.
6. An even multiple of 10 down.
7. A multiple of half the number formed by the first two digits of 2 down.
9. The square of the cube root of 6 down.
11. The same when reversed.
13. All digits odd and all different.

DOWN

2. When reversed this is the square of a prime number.
3. The sum of the digits is greater than 39.
4. A square. The sum of the digits is greater than 10.
6. The cube of the square root of 9 across.

8. Digits of 4 down rearranged.
10. A prime number.
12. Either this number or this number reversed is either a multiple or a factor of the number formed by the first two digits of 2 down.

PART SEVEN

Some Orders of Merit

65—74

65. Mathematics, English and French

A class of 23 is placed in order (no ties) for three different subjects — Mathematics, English and French. The marks for the three subjects are then added up and a combined order is produced. (No information is given about the ranges of the marks for the three subjects.)

	Mathematics	*English*	*French*	*Combined*
(i)	1	1	1	–
(ii)	1	–	1	1
(iii)	2	5	6	–
(iv)	17	21	23	–
(v)	17	19	–	1

In line (i) we suppose that a man was 1st for Mathematics, 1st for English and 1st for French. *What, if anything, can be said about his place for the three subjects combined?* In line (ii) we suppose that a man was 1st for Mathematics, 1st for French and 1st for the three subjects combined. *What, if anything, can be said about his place for English?* Similarly you are asked to give what information you can about the missing places in lines (iii), (iv) and (v).

66. The Deception Test

Another order of merit (no ties) for A, B, C, D, E — this time for Deception. In their usual chatty way they are making remarks about their places. The remarks of those who were first and second are false, the rest are true.

A: D was third.
B: E was not first.
C: I was not last.
D: C was lower than B.
E: B was second.

What were their places?

67. Who Beat Whom?

A, B, C, D, E all know their own places in an order of merit (no ties) and B also knows D's place.

A: 'I was not second.'
B: 'I was two places higher than D.'

C overheard these remarks and on the evidence of what he knew about their characters came to the conclusion that one of them was true and the other false. (He was quite right.)

After a pause for reflection C announced that he could write down the complete order of merit of all five of them. He did so, and he was quite right. With the additional information that C was not 5th you should be able to *discover the complete order of merit.*

68. The Race is to the Ruthless

Alf, Bert, Charlie, Duggie and Ernie are placed in an order of merit once more (no ties), this time for Ruthlessness. Charlie and Duggie are next to each other in the order and they each make two remarks. Those made by the one who was higher are both false, those made by the other are both true.

CHARLIE: 1. Ernie's place was half way between those of Bert and Charlie.
2. Duggie was 3rd.

DUGGIE: 1. Alf's place was half way between those of Charlie and Ernie.
2. Bert was higher than Alf and Charlie.

What is the order of merit?

69. The Brainstorm Brothers

The five Brainstorm brothers — Clarence, Claud, Casanova, Charles and Terence — are placed in an order of merit (no ties) for quickness in the uptake.

They all know their own places and Casanova has also been informed that Charles was two places higher than Clarence.

Casanova says: 'If I make what seems to me the reasonable assumption that Terence can't possibly have been first, I can tell you the order of merit for all five of us.'

This 'reasonable assumption' is in fact perfectly correct.

What is the order of merit?

70. The Efficiency Test

Alf, Bert, Charlie, Duggie and Ernie are making predictions about the order in which they will be placed for their coming efficiency test.

They speak as follows:

ALF: Bert will be two places higher than Charlie.
BERT: I will be third.
CHARLIE: Duggie will be first.
DUGGIE: Bert will be second.
ERNIE: Charlie will be three places lower than Alf.

It was interesting to see, after the test was over, that of these predictions only one was right, and that was made by the person who was first.

What were their places in the test? (There were no ties.)

71. Bert goes Psychic

Alf, Bert, Charlie, Duggie and Ernie have just been undergoing a test, as a result of which they are placed in an order of merit (no ties). They are all told their own places but none of them is told anything about anyone else's place.

Alf said that he wasn't second, and Bert, who has recently been claiming to be psychic, announced with closed eyes and a curious expression on his face that he felt sure he was two places higher than Duggie. Charlie overheard these remarks and came to the conclusion — for reasons that need not concern us — that one of them was right and the other wrong.

After a pause for reflection Charlie, who is an intelligent person, said that he could announce the correct order of merit for all five of them. But when he did so he had got everyone in the wrong place except the last two.

Find the correct order.

(It is pleasant to record that Alf and Bert are placed in the order of their truthfulness.)

72. The Ladies' Tests

Priscilla, Queenie and Rachel have been placed in an order of merit (no ties) for Charm, Femininity and Intuition. To start off with they each know all their own places, but none of the places of the others. Priscilla, however, is unable to keep a secret and she says: 'I was higher for Femininity than I was for Charm or Intuition.' Queenie, who is an intelligent young lady then says: 'In that case I know all our places for each of the three subjects.'

With the information that Rachel is higher for Charm than for Intuition you too should be able to *discover the order of merit for each test.*

73. Latin, Greek and Mathematics

A, B, C, D, E are placed in an order of merit, (no ties), at Latin, Greek and Mathematics. In no case is the order completely alphabetical. You are told that:

(i) A is higher at Latin than D is at Greek, but A is not top at Latin, and D is not bottom at Greek.

(ii) B's average place is 3rd, and he wasn't top at anything.

(iii) C is higher at Mathematics than at Latin, and higher at Latin than at Greek.

(iv) E's Mathematics place is lower than his Latin place, and his Latin place is lower than C's Greek place.

(v) The sum of D's places is 3 more than the sum of C's.

Find the order in each subject.

74. Honesty, Intelligence and Charm

Alf, Bert, Charlie, Duggie and Ernie are arranged in an order of merit (no ties) for Honesty, Charm and Intelligence. In the remarks which they make about the places of themselves and others, those who are 1st, 2nd or 3rd for Honesty invariably tell the truth, but all the remarks made by the other two are false.

ALF: (i) Duggie was 1st for Honesty.
(ii) I was not higher for Charm than I was for Intelligence.

BERT: (i) I was higher for Intelligence than I was for Honesty
(ii) I was higher for Charm than I was for Intelligence.

CHARLIE: (i) I was 4th for Honesty.
(ii) I was not higher for Intelligence than I was for Charm.

DUGGIE: (i) Alf was 4th for Honesty.
(ii) In at least one test Ernie was lower than Charlie.

ERNIE: (i) I was 3rd for Charm.
(ii) The sum of the numbers of Duggie's places is one less than the sum of the numbers of Bert's.

Find the order of merit in each of the three tests.

PART EIGHT

Our Factory

75—86

75. Cousins and Uncles

They always talked about themselves in our factory as one big happy family, and that is in fact literally true. Alf, Bert, Charlie, Duggie, Ernie, Fred and George can all be represented on one family tree such that every male who appears on the tree is one of the seven. Their jobs are, not necessarily respectively, Door-Shutter, Door-Opener, Door-Knob-Polisher, Sweeper-Upper, Bottle-Washer, Welfare Officer and Worker. Except for Charlie, who remains silent, they all make remarks, which are true, as follows:

ALF: 1. My brother-in-law is the Welfare Officer.

BERT: 1. My father's brother is George's sister's father-in-law.
2. My brother is the Door-Opener.

DUGGIE: 1. My father is the Bottle-Washer.
2. Ernie's son is the Door-Shutter.

ERNIE: 1. Duggie's brother is the Door-Knob-Polisher.
2. My father is the Worker.

FRED: 1. My nephew is the Door-Shutter.

GEORGE: 1. Bert is the Door-Shutter's cousin.

Find their jobs and how they are all related to each other.

76. Higher Thinking by Alf and Ernie

Alf, Bert, Charlie, Duggie and Ernie have just been having a test for the new instant thinking and they are placed in an order of merit (no ties). Each man knows his own place and that Duggie was 2 places higher than Bert.

Alf says: 'If I knew whether Charlie was first, I would know everyone's place'.

Ernie, who has heard this remark, says: 'That informs me whether Charlie was first. I know everyone's place'.

Find the order of merit.

77. Personnel Tests in the Factory

In the days when they were still the only five employees in our Factory, Alf, Bert, Charlie, Duggie and Ernie were required to undergo tests for Aplomb, for Integrity, and for Occupational Mobility. In each test they were placed in an order of merit (no ties). They were informed about their own places, but not about anybody else's.

Alf remarked that he was higher for Aplomb than he was for Integrity, and higher for Integrity than for Occupational Mobility.

Bert said that his places were all different and that he wasn't top or bottom for anything.

Charlie, on the other hand, said that he was either top or bottom in each test.

Duggie, who had been listening carefully to these remarks and who was in fact first for Aplomb, but not first or last for anything else, then announced that if he knew whether Charlie was top for Integrity he could tell the exact order in each test.

We are not prepared to reveal this, but if we tell you instead that Ernie was one place higher for Integrity than Duggie you should be able to *discover all their places in each test.*

78. Intellectual Awareness

Alf, Bert, Charlie, Duggie and Ernie have once more been indulging their insatiable urge for competition. This time they have been competing against each other for Intellectual Awareness — with the Managing Director of course as judge. As a result they are placed in an order of merit (no ties).

Alf says: 'I know Bert's place as well as my own — I was higher than he was — but no one else's. If I knew that Charlie was three places higher than Duggie — which is about what I would expect — I would know the places of all five of us.'

Ernie, who has been listening to Alf's remarks, has been told no one's place except his own. But he feels quite confident that, as he puts it; 'The half-witted and incompetent Duggie could not possibly have been higher than Bert.' (He was quite right — Duggie was not higher than Bert). After a pause for reflection Ernie says: 'I can now write down all our places.'

He does so, and he is quite right.

What was the order of merit?

79. An Intelligence Test in the Factory

My old friends Alf, Bert, Charlie, Duggie and Ernie have just been placed in an order of merit for an intelligence test (no ties).

They made various remarks — not unfortunately all true — about the places of themselves and others. On examining these remarks I noticed the curious fact that if the speaker was placed higher in the order of merit than the person or persons mentioned the remark was true, if the speaker was placed lower than the person or persons mentioned the remark was false. When two people were mentioned, in no case was the speaker between them.

As I do not propose to reveal to you which remarks were made by which person I have called the speakers P, Q, R, S, T in no particular order. (Remarks that the speaker makes about himself are all made in the first person.)

P: I was higher than Bert and Charlie.

Q: 1. Neither Alf nor Charlie was 5th.
  2. Ernie was 2nd.

R: Charlie was higher than Ernie.

S: Duggie was 1st.

T: 1. Ernie was 4th.
  2. Charlie was lower than Alf.

Find the identities of P, Q, R, S, T and the order of merit.

80. The Birthday Kings

Alf, Bert, Charlie, Duggie and Ernie have recently discovered the remarkable fact that all their birthdays are on the same day, though their ages are all different. On their mutual birthday (when their ages of course are all an exact number of years) they are having a typically inconsequential conversation about it. Here are some of the things that I overheard:

Alf said to Bert: 'Your age is exactly 70 per cent greater than mine.'

Bert said to Charlie: (i) 'Ernie is younger than you.' (ii) 'The difference between your age and Duggie's is the same as the difference between Duggie's and Ernie's.'

Charlie said to Alf: (i) 'I'm 10 years older than you.' (ii) 'Bert is younger than Duggie.'

Charlie said to Duggie: 'The difference between my age and yours is 6 years.'

Duggie said to Bert: 'I'm 9 years older than Ernie.'

Ernie said to Bert: 'I'm 7 years older than Alf.'

Knowing all their ages as I do I realised at once that they were not all telling the truth. On analysing their remarks I discovered the interesting fact that when speaking to someone older than themselves everything they said was true, but when speaking to someone younger everything they said was false.

Find all their ages.

81. Holidays Abroad

Alf, Bert, Charlie, Duggie and Ernie went with their wives for holidays abroad last year. Boulogne, Calais and Dunkirk were the rather unenterprising destinations of three of the pairs, but the other two ventured further afield to Andorra and Ethiopia. I knew that the names of the five wives were Agnes, Beatrice, Clarissa, Daphne and Ethel, but the only information I had about who was married to whom was that for each pair the names of the husband, the wife and last year's holiday destination all began with different letters.

In an attempt to discover rather more I had some conversation with three of the ladies.

Beatrice told me that she was not married to Alf and that she had heard from Ernie that Charlie went to Dunkirk last year.

Daphne, however, firmly informed me that Charlie went to Ethiopia and that Beatrice went to Dunkirk. 'Unlike some people I could mention,' she added darkly, but rather irrelevantly, 'Alf always tells the truth.'

Clarissa said that when her husband was asked whether Ethel was married to Charlie he replied 'No'. She went on to tell me that Duggie went to Boulogne.

When I had been told from another source the curious fact that of each of these married couples one member always told the truth and the other never did, I was able to deduce the name of each man's wife and where they all went for their holidays.

Can you?

82. Our Factory at Ascot

A glorious Saturday in June found the employees in our factory at Ascot. Alf, Bert, Charlie, Duggie, Ernie, Fred and George had with them their wives who are called, not respectively, Agnes, Beatrice, Clarissa, Daisy, Ermyntrude, Flossie and Gertie.

The wives are wearing, again not respectively, most elegant hats which are florally decorated with Aspidistras, Begonias, Crocuses, Dahlias, Edelweiss, Fuchsias and Gentians.

Each lady's husband and flower have different initial letters which are not the same as the initial letter of the lady's name.

Each of the 14 people either always tells the truth or never does. Of each married couple one member and one only is a liar.

The men are all speechless with emotion and fatigue and their wives do the talking, as follows:

AGNES:
1. When asked whether Gertie was wearing a Fuchsia hat George said *No*.
2. When asked whether Ernie's wife was wearing a Begonia hat Duggie said *Yes*.
3. When asked whether Beatrice was wearing a Fuchsia hat Clarissa said *Yes*.

BEATRICE:
1. Alf is not married to Ermyntrude.
2. When asked whether Fred was married to Gertie Clarissa's husband said *Yes*.
3. When asked whether George's wife was wearing a Fuchsia hat Fred said *Yes*.

CLARISSA:
1. Daisy is wearing a Begonia hat.
2. My husband is George.
3. Ermyntrude's husband is a liar.

DAISY:
1. When asked whether Duggie was married to Clarissa Alf said *Yes*.
2. Ernie is a liar.
3. Fred's wife is wearing a Crocus hat.

ERMYNTRUDE:
1. Alf always tells the truth.

2. Charlie's wife is not wearing an Edelweiss hat.
3. When asked whether she was Ernie's wife Clarissa said *No*.

FLOSSIE:
1. Duggie's wife is wearing an Aspidistra hat.
2. When asked whether Daisy was Bert's wife my husband said *No*.

GERTIE:
1. When asked whether Flossie was wearing a Begonia hat Bert said *Yes*.
2. Bert's wife is wearing an Aspidistra hat.

Find for each man his wife's name and the floral decoration in her hat, and find which of the 14 tell the truth and which tell lies.

83. Our Factory on the Cricket Field

We are all keen, and most of us active, cricketers. In one of our tea-breaks the other day Alf, Bert, Charlie, Duggie and Ernie were discussing their last match. Four of them had been playing for the factory side and one had been umpiring. Of the four players one was an opening bat (who did not bowl), one the wicket-keeper (who also of course did not bowl), one a fast bowler and the other a leg-break bowler. It was a one-innings match in which no individual scored more than 100 runs.

The umpire of course always tells the truth, and so does the wicket-keeper. The leg-break bowler has been trained in the ways of deception and never tells the truth, the fast bowler and the opening batsman make statements which are alternately true and false, or false and true.

They speak as follows:

ALF:
1. Ernie is not the leg-break bowler.
2. Charlie's score is not a multiple of 9.
3. Two of the opposition were run out.

BERT:
1. Charlie's score was a multiple of 7.
2. Duggie scored twice as many as Alf and Bert between them.
3. Duggie scored 10 per cent more than Charlie.

CHARLIE:
1. The fast bowler and the leg-break bowler took the same number of wickets.
2. Duggie's score was a perfect square.

DUGGIE:
1. Charlie took four wickets.
2. Charlie scored less than Bert.
3. Ernie took five wickets.
4. I scored exactly as many as two of the others between them.
5. Alf was the wicket-keeper.

ERNIE:
1. Duggie was not the umpire.
2. Duggie took more than three wickets.
3. Alf scored 37.

4. Bert scored eight times as many runs as the fast bowler took wickets.

Who did what, and how many runs and wickets, if any, did each of them get?

84. Our Factory at Suez

I am proud to say that at the time of the Suez crisis our friends responded with typical alacrity and patriotism to the call of the United Nations and moved swiftly out to help salvage the Canal.

It will be remembered that their names are Alf, Bert, Charlie, Duggie, Ernie, Fred and George and that their jobs used to be, not necessarily respectively, Door-Opener, Door-Shutter, Door-Knob-Polisher, Sweeper-Upper, Bottle-Washer, Welfare Officer and Worker. (Their jobs just before the Suez crisis were not necessarily the same as in any other example.)

They are nothing if not adaptable and they realised that new conditions called for new tasks. Their new jobs were, again not necessarily respectively:

P.R.O.U.N. (Public Relations Officer United Nations)
P.E. (Propaganda Executive)
G.D.O. (Garbage-Disposal Officer)
W.D.L. (Wreck-Detection Lieutenant)
W.D. (Water-Diviner (in case they can't find the canal))
Frogman
N.B.W. (New Bottle-Washer (as this is one thing they can't do without))

They gave a collective interview in Suez to the Press of the World. They were prepared to divulge what their old jobs were but for Security reasons their names and their new jobs can only be discovered by the use of reason.

They say:

DOOR-OPENER:	My name is George.
DOOR-SHUTTER:	1. Alf is the P.E.
	2. Ernie is not the G.D.O.
	3. Fred is the N.B.W.
WELFARE OFFICER:	The G.D.O. used to have one of the door jobs.
DOOR-KNOB-POLISHER:	1. Bert was not the old B.W.
	2. The W.D.L. is the old Door-Opener.
SWEEPER-UPPER:	1. My name is Duggie.
	2. George is the G.D.O.
BOTTLE-WASHER:	1. The P.E. used to be the Sweeper-Upper.
	2. Charlie is the Frogman.
WORKER:	1. I am the G.D.O.
	2. Charlie used to be the Door-Opener.

Any remark of which the subject comes after the speaker in the alphabet is true; if the subject comes before the speaker it is false, e.g. if Charlie makes a remark about Ernie it is true, if about Bert it is false.

Remarks about themselves are always made in the first person.

Anything that the Water-Diviner, Frogman, New Bottle-Washer say about themselves is true. Anything that anybody else says about themselves is false.

Find all their names and their new occupations.

85. Names, Names, Names

The following interesting facts about the other names of Alf, Bert, Charlie and Duggie have not, I think, previously been revealed. They have as their second names, Algernon, Basil, Claude and Desmond; as their third names Aaron, Balaam, Cain and David; and their surnames are Angle, Bangle, Congle and Dongle. (In every case these names are *not necessarily respectively.*)

They each make two remarks, as shown below. If and only if a man makes two true remarks he is 'perfect' (i.e. his four names begin with four different letters.)

If and only if a man makes two false remarks he is 'imperfect' (i.e. his four names begin with the same letter.)

(In no case does anyone have exactly *three* names beginning with the same letter.)

ALF: 1. Bert is Basil.
2. Charlie is 'perfect'.

BERT: 1. Balaam is 'perfect'.
2. Alf is Claude.

CHARLIE: 1. Alf is 'imperfect'.
2. Bert is not Basil.

DUGGIE: 1. Claude is not Aaron.
2. David is not Dongle.

Find the other names of Alf, Bert, Charlie and Duggie.

86. How Old?

Alf knows, as everyone else does, that Bert must be over 20 — otherwise of course he wouldn't have been allowed to join our staff, but he is very anxious to discover *exactly* how old Bert is. Pausing sometimes for thought and calculation on hearing the answers, Alf asks Bert the following questions:

1. Is your age a multiple of 17?
2. Is it a multiple of 3?
3. Is it a prime number?
4. Are you older than I am? (Bert knows Alf's age.)
5. Have you had your 51st birthday?

Alf then claims that he knows Bert's age and he announces it. But he is wrong.

Charlie has overheard this conversation and from it he is able to deduce Alf's age correctly. From his knowledge of Bert's character he guesses that he has given answers that are alternately true and false. Charlie's own age is a prime number, and he knows that Bert is older than he is. But, although he has guessed correctly how *many* of Bert's answers are false he has got the wrong ones, and so it is not surprising that when he announces what he claims to be Bert's age he too is wrong.

Duggie who has also overheard what has been going on is rather shrewder than Charlie and he guesses correctly which of Bert's answers were false. And, as he knows that Bert is younger than he is, he is able to announce Bert's age correctly. Duggie's age is a multiple of 13.

How old are Alf, Bert, Charlie and Duggie?
(Their ages are all different.)

PART NINE

The Island of Imperfection

87—91

87. Tom, Dick and Harry

There are three tribes on the Island of Imperfection — the Pukkas who always tell the truth, the Wotta-Woppas who never tell the truth, and the Shilli-Shallas who make statements which are alternately true and false or false and true.

An explorer lands on the island and questions three natives — Tom, Dick and Harry, — as follows:

He asks Tom: Which tribe do you belong to?

Tom answers: I'm a Pukka.

He asks Dick: (i) Which tribe do you belong to?

Dick answers: I'm a Wotta-Woppa.

(ii) Was Tom telling the truth?

Dick answers: Yes.

He asks Harry: (i) Which tribe do you belong to?

Harry answers: I'm a Pukka.

(ii) Which tribe does Tom belong to?

Harry answers: He's a Shilli-Shalla.

To which tribe does each man belong?

88. Awful, Beastly, Chronic and Dim

Everyone on the Island of Imperfection belongs to one of three tribes: the Pukkas, who always tell the truth; the Wotta-Woppas, who never tell the truth; and the Shilli-Shallas, who make statements which are alternately true and false (or false and true).

Four male members of the Island — Awful, Beastly, Chronic and Dim — make statements as follows:

AWFUL: 1. Beastly owes me ten rats.
2. Chronic is a Pukka.
3. Beastly is a Pukka.
4. Dim owes me five rats.

BEASTLY: 1. Chronic is a Wotta-Woppa.
2. I do not owe Awful ten rats.
3. Dim has three wives.
4. Chronic owes me fifteen rats.

CHRONIC: 1. I am the weakest man on the island.
2. I am the poorest man on the island.
3. I am the ugliest man on the island.
4. I have 5 wives.

DIM: 1. I am not a Pukka.
2. I do not owe Awful five rats.
3. Chronic is not a Shilla-Shalla.
4. Chronic is a bachelor.

Find the tribes to which these four men belong, and which of these statements are true and which false.

89. Monogamy Comes to the Island

All the inhabitants of the island are still members of one of three tribes — the Pukkas, who always tell the truth; the Shilli-Shallas, who make statements which are alternately true and false (or false and true); and the Wotta-Woppas, who never tell the truth.

To prevent the unsatisfactory results of inbreeding it has recently been decreed that there should be no marriages between people of the same tribe. It has also been laid down that in future there shall be one man — one wife.

The ladies have cheered up considerably now that they are to have a husband each. The four with whom our story deals are called Eager, Frolic, Glorious and Happy. The names of their husbands, not necessarily respectively, are Sordid, Tired, Under and Venal.

The men have not been talking much recently, and the ladies speak as follows:

EAGER: 1. Sordid is married to Glorious.
2. Sordid is a Wotta-Woppa.
3. Venal is not a Wotta-Woppa.

FROLIC: 1. Glorious is not a Pukka.
2. My husband is a Pukka.
3. My husband is Tired.

GLORIOUS: 1. Happy is married to a Wotta-Woppa.
2. Under is a Pukka.
3. Eager is a Wotta-Woppa.

HAPPY: 1. Frolic is a Pukka.
2. Glorious is a Wotta-Woppa.
3. Eager is a Shilli-Shalla.

Find who is married to whom, and the tribes to which they all belong.

90. Discontent in the Island

Many years have passed since monogamy was introduced, and the ladies have discovered the hard way that the fewer the wives the more the household chores that have to be done by each.

Our story deals with the four Dis sisters (Dis-Appointed, Dis-Enchanted, Dis-Illusioned and Dis-Tressed), their four husbands and one son from each of the four large families. The husbands' names are Peter, Quintin, Ronald, and Simon, and the names of the four sons are Willy, Xerxes, Younger and Zacharias (in both cases in no particular order).

It will be remembered that everyone on the island belongs to one of three tribes — the Pukkas, who always tell the truth; the Wotta-Woppas, who never tell the truth; and the Shilli-Shallas who make statements which are alternately true and false (or false and true). It will also be remembered that when monogamy was introduced it was decreed that there should be no marriages between members of the same tribe.

Over the years an exceedingly interesting biological fact has emerged, namely that the children of a marriage never belong to the tribe of either their mother or their father.

The ladies are still doing most of the talking. They speak as follows:

DIS-APPOINTED:
1. Zacharias is Ronald's son.
2. Simon is Xerxes' father.
3. Younger is a Wotta-Woppa.

DIS-ENCHANTED:
1. Xerxes is a Pukka.
2. Illusioned is a Shilli-Shalla.
3. Xerxes is not my son.

DIS-ILLUSIONED:
1. Tressed is not a Pukka.
2. My son is a Pukka.
3. I am married to a Wotta-Woppa.

DIS-TRESSED:
1. Enchanted is a Wotta-Woppa.
2. I am married to Simon.

3. Enchanted and Quintin belong to the same tribe.

Find the names of the father and the mother of each boy, and find to which tribe all twelve people belong.

91. All this and Football too

The Islanders have only recently taken up Association Football, but they have already organised themselves into four teams. One team consists only of Pukkas, who always tell the truth; another team consists only of Wotta-Woppas, who never tell the truth; the third team consists only of Shilli-Shallas, who make statements which are alternately true and false, or false and true; and the fourth team (the Cocktail team) contains members of all three tribes. The four teams are also denoted by the letters A, B, C, D, in no particular order.

Peter, Quintin, Rupert, Sam and Tom are all members of one of these teams, and of course they are all members of one of the three tribes on the island. (All the four teams do not necessarily have a member among these five young gentlemen. But no team has more than two of them as members.)

The four teams all played each other once. After the matches were over Peter, Quintin, Rupert, Sam and Tom spoke as follows:

PETER:
1. I am in the Cocktail team.
2. Quintin plays for the Wotta-Woppa team.
3. Rupert's team beat Tom's team 4–0.
4. Rupert plays for the Shilli-Shalla team.
5. B scored 2 goals against C.

QUINTIN:
1. B is the Wotta-Woppa team.
2. Tom is a Pukka.
3. Tom is a Wotta-Woppa.
4. Peter is not a Pukka.

5. B's goal average is better than C's.

RUPERT: 1. B scored 3 goals altogether.

2. The match between C and D was a draw.

3. I am not a member of C.

4. B beat D.

SAM: 1. A is the Wotta-Woppa team.

2. D scored more goals against B than they did against A.

3. I play for A.

4. B did not win any of their matches.

TOM: 1. D is not the Cocktail team.

2. C drew two matches.

3. Peter plays for the Pukka team.

4. D scored 3 goals altogether.

5. C's goal average is better than B's.

There is no match in which the total of goals scored reaches double figures.

Find which team is the representative of each tribe and which is the Cocktail team. Find also to which tribe each man belongs, which team he plays for, and the score in each match. (A side's goal average is the ratio of total goals for to total goals against).

PART TEN

Miscellaneous — Hard

92—101

92. Clubs and Careers

Algernon, Basil, Clarence, Douglas and Ethelred are members, not necessarily respectively of five different clubs — the Boojums, the Amalgamated Brick Droppers, the Simpler Life, the Better Life and the Longer Life. Their professions are, again not necessarily respectively, Advertising Consultant, Sales Promoter, Purchase Adviser, Profit Calculator and Garbage Collector. In no case does anyone know the profession or the club of any of the others before our story starts.

And then, when they are all collected together they begin to talk.

Algernon says that he is not a member of the Amalgamated Brick Droppers and that he is not a Sales Promoter. Basil says that he does not belong to the Simpler Life and is not a Profit Calculator. Douglas says that he too is not a member of the Simpler Life and also is not a Sales Promoter. Clarence has been listening to these remarks with his usual care and intelligence and says: 'If I knew that the person who is a member of Simpler Life was a Sales Promoter I would know for certain that Algernon was a member either of Boojums or of Longer Life, and that Basil was either an Advertising Consultant or a Purchase Adviser.'

Ethelred has also been listening carefully and he is, if possible even more intelligent than Clarence. He says: 'Douglas must be a member either of Boojums or of Longer Life, but I don't know which. And Douglas must be either the Profit Calculator or the Purchase Adviser.'

With the additional information that the Purchase Adviser is not a member of the Simpler Life, and that the Sales Promoter is not a member of Boojums, you should be able to *find all their clubs and professions*.

93. The Car of Jones

Smith is anxious to know the registration number of Jones's car. He doesn't even know how many figures it contains, but he has reason to believe (and he is quite right) that it is less than 9200.

Smith knows that Jones is in the habit of making statements which are alternately true and false, but unfortunately he has been misinformed about the truthfulness of the statement by Jones which immediately preceded his (Smith's) questions to him. Smith writes down on a sheet of paper three questions to which he asks Jones to write down answers, Yes or No:

The questions are:

1. Is the number a perfect square?
2. Is it a multiple of 19?
3. Is it the product of 5 different primes (excluding 1)?

After reading what Jones has written and after a decent pause for reflection and calculation Smith has no reason to change his views about which answers are true and which false. He says: 'If I knew that there was at least one nought in it I could tell you the number.' He is told, truthfully, that there is *not* a nought in it.

What was the number of Jones's car?

94. Pongle and Quongle play Football

Pongle, Quongle, Robinson, Smith and Tigger are members, not necessarily respectively, of five different football teams, A, B, C, D, E who all played each other once in a competition. They make remarks as follows. (If a person makes a remark in which his own team is mentioned it is *false*. Otherwise it is *true*.)

PONGLE:
1. The score in A *v.* C was 2–0.
2. C drew 2 matches.
3. E scored no goals.
4. B was the only side to score against A.

QUONGLE:
1. The score in B *v.* D was 3–1.
2. D scored 9 goals altogether.
3. B scored altogether 1 goal more than C.

ROBINSON:
1. C scored 7 goals altogether.
2. B beat C.
3. C scored 3 goals against D.
4. A scored twice as many goals as were scored against them.

SMITH:
1. The score in D *v.* B was 1–3.
2. C did not beat E.
3. The score in B *v.* A was 2–1.
4. The score in C *v.* D was 2–2.

TIGGER:
1. The score in B *v.* D was 3–1.
2. E did not lose to C.
3. B only had 2 goals scored against them.
4. D only lost 1 match.

Find the team to which each person belongs, and the score in each match.

95. Frocks for the Frolic

Five young ladies, Priscilla, Queenie, Rachel, Sybil and Tess, were discussing what their frocks should be made of for the forthcoming frolic.

Priscilla says: 'I will wear lace unless Rachel wears muslin and Sybil does not wear nylon, in which case I will wear organdie, but not otherwise.'

Queenie, who is rather bossy says: 'Rachel must wear nylon unless Tess wears lace (in which case Rachel must wear organdie) or unless Tess wears muslin (in which case Rachel must wear muslin too).

Rachel says: 'I will wear lace unless Sybil wears muslin'.

Sybil says: 'If Priscilla wears lace then I will wear organdie.'

Tess says to Queenie: 'If Priscilla does not wear lace you will wear either lace or muslin — whichever of these two is worn less by the rest of us.'

These remarks seem to be a happy blend of predictions, commands and expressions of intention. But, whichever they were, it is pleasant to record that they were all obeyed or proved to be true.

What did the young ladies wear at the frolic?

96. The Five Discs

(This is an adaptation in a more complicated form of a famous 'three discs' problem.)

There are five men A, B, C, D, E, each wearing a disc on his forehead selected from a total of five white, two red and two black. Each man can see the colours of the discs worn by the other four, but he is unable to see his own. They are all intelligent people, and they are asked to try to deduce the colour of their own disc from the colours of the other four that they see. In fact they are all wearing white discs. After a pause for reflection C, who is even more intelligent than the others, says, 'I reckon I must be wearing a white disc.'

By what process of reasoning could he have arrived at this conclusion?

97. Time Trouble

Alf, Bert, Charlie and Duggie were the first to volunteer for the British satellite. At the time with which our story was concerned they were moving through space at a speed and in a direction such that the hands of their special chronometer which allowed for local variations in time had, since they left, been moving exactly twice as fast as those of the Greenwich Mean Time clock.

Any references to the passing of time as recorded by the G.M.T. clock are in italics thus: *time*, *hours*, *minutes* etc., and any references to the time recorded by the satellite chronometer are in ordinary letters.

They speak:

DUGGIE: O Alf, O Bert! that all should come to this!
In less than half an hour tomorrow's here,
And our today is one with yesteryear.

ALF: Yes, your today perhaps, but not so mine!
You watch the clock; myself I watch the *time*.
10 minutes since I heard the *hour* strike.

And in another *23 minutes* it will be 2½ hours after that moment, 34 minutes before we set off, when Charlie lost his bike.

BERT: *tomorrow* and tomorrow and *tomorrow*!
When will they both arrive? More than *2 hours* alas!
Before the *time* is what the time is now
Just *half an hour* must pass.
O, Alf and Charlie pray
That you'll repent ere then
the lies you've told this day.
(In case I fail to make my meaning plain,
You're liars both. Try not to lie again!)

CHARLIE: I'm not a very clever chap.
I cannot tell the time.
I cannot add, nor yet subtract,

I'm not much good at rhyme.
I never learnt much really. Some say that I'm uncouth.
But unlike Bert and Duggie, Alf and I do tell the truth.

There is a 5 *minute* pause for reflection between the above speeches.

For each speaker either everything he says is true or everything he says is false.

What was the G.M.T. when they started?

98. Salamanca Street

Gongle, Hongle and Ian live in three different houses (between numbers 13 and 99 inclusive) in Salamanca Street. John is an old friend who is staying with Gongle.

Gongle, Ian and John do not know the number of Hongle's house, but they all four of them know the numbers of Gongle's and Ian's (Ian lives in number 49; the number of Gongle's house is odd, and is less than that of Ian's).

Gongle asks Hongle the following questions about the number of his house:

1. Is the number of your house bigger than that of mine?
2. Is it bigger than that of Ian's?
3. Is it a perfect square?
4. Is it divisible by 3?

Ian and John hear these questions and the answers which Hongle gives.

Gongle thinks that Hongle's answers are all true. Whatever Ian thinks is true in Hongle's answers, John thinks is false, and *vice versa*. John thinks that only Hongle's second answer is true. Hongle's answers are in fact alternately 'Yes' and 'No', but you are not told which comes first.

After a pause for thought Gongle, Ian and John all say that they know the number of Hongle's house, but when asked what it is their answers are all wrong.

Karl, who has been listening, does not live in Salamanca Street. He is informed by Hongle that only two of his answers are true, and Hongle tells him which. Karl, who already knows the numbers of Gongle's and Ian's houses is then able to announce the number of Hongle's house correctly.

What are the numbers of Gongle's and Hongle's houses?

What were the incorrect numbers of Hongle's house given by Gongle, Ian and John?

99. Round the Bend

If one goes round the Centenary Corner in Calculation Crescent one comes to a group of new houses, numbered from 101 to 200 inclusive, which are reserved for higher mathematicians only. The three Fraction brothers — Proper, Improper and Vulgar — have recently moved into separate houses here, but they none of them know where either of the others live. They all take the view that mathematical information should be earned, and not given away.

Proper, however, has persuaded Vulgar to write down the answers to three questions about the number of his house.

They are: 1. Is your number a square?
2. Is it a cube?
3. Is it a multiple of 29?

Proper reads the answers and says, 'If I knew that your number was greater than 150 I could tell you what it is.'

Improper has read the questions and answers, and has heard Proper's comment. From his observations along the road he has reason to believe that Vulgar's number is less than 150, and that the difference between the number of his house and that of Proper's is less than 30. After a little thought he claims to be able to write down the numbers of the other two houses. He does so, but only Proper's number is correct, which is not surprising considering that only Vulgar's answer to question (2) was true, and that his belief that Vulgar's number was less than 150 was incorrect.

What are the numbers of the houses of Proper, Improper and Vulgar?

100. The Island of Indecision

Each inhabitant of the Island of Indecision belongs to one of four tribes:

The Nevahs, who never tell the truth;

the Oddfellahs, who only tell the truth on days which are odd-numbered dates of the month;

the Pickahs, who only tell the truth on Wednesdays and Fridays;

the Quaints, who always tell the truth except on Mondays and Thursdays, when they make statements which are alternately true and false.

Algernon, Basil, Clarence, Donald and Ernest are five inhabitants of the island who make statements as follows:

ALGERNON: (i) Today is the 14th.
(ii) Basil is an Oddfellah.

BASIL: (i) Today is the 13th.
(ii) Ernest is a Nevah.
(iii) I am an Oddfellah.

CLARENCE: (i) Today is Monday.
(ii) Ernest is a Pickah.
(iii) Basil is a Pickah.

DONALD: (i) Basil is not a Quaint.
(ii) Yesterday was the 15th.
(iii) Clarence is a Pickah.
(iv) Today is Monday.

ERNEST: (i) Tomorrow is not Wednesday.
(ii) Algernon is not a Quaint.
(iii) Algernon belongs to the same tribe as Donald.

Find the tribe to which each person belongs, and find also the day of the week and the date of the month.

101. Calculation Crescent

CLARENCE: Like you and me, Cuthbert, those three people all live in Calculation Crescent, and the numbers of their houses add up to twice the number of your house. Multiplied together their three numbers make 1260. The numbers of our five houses are, of course, all different.

CUTHBERT: That doesn't tell me what their numbers are.

CLARENCE: That's true. But it will if I give you the additional information that the number of my house is greater than that of any of yours.

Calculation Crescent has houses numbered, rather curiously, from 2 to 222.

Find the numbers of the houses of Clarence, Cuthbert and the three people they are talking about.

Solutions

1. Wedding Predictions

1. Since the only one to predict correctly was the man who married Prudence, ∴ John did not predict correctly (that Arthur would marry Prudence). ∴ Arthur did not marry Prudence, and John did not marry Prudence.

2. ∴ Arthur did not predict correctly. ∴ David married Eve.

3. ∴ by elimination Prudence married George. ∴ George and only George predicted correctly.

4. ∴ John did not marry Christine. ∴ by elimination Arthur married Christine, and John married Rose.

Complete result: George married Prudence; John married Rose; Arthur married Christine; David married Eve.

Arsenal did *not* win the F.A. Cup.

2. The Engine-driver's Shirt

Diagram:

	Red	Blue	Black	Green	E-driver	Stoker	Guard	Porter
Smith			×	×			×	
Brown					×			
Jones				×				×
Robinson								
E-driver	×							
Stoker	√	×	×	×				
Guard	×		×	×				
Porter	×			×				

1. Fill in information given.

i. Engine driver not Brown.

ii. Smith not Guard; neither Smith nor Guard wore black or green shirts.

iii. Jones not Porter; neither Jones nor Porter wore green shirt.

iv. Stoker wore red shirt. ∴ Stoker wore no other colour shirt, and no one else wore red shirt.

(This information has been inserted in diagram; other information should be inserted as discovered.)

2. From diagram, by elimination, Engine driver wore green shirt; Porter wore black shirt; Guard wore blue shirt.

3. Engine driver wore green; but neither Smith nor Jones wore green, ∴ Engine driver not Smith or Jones. ∴ Engine driver Robinson, and since Engine driver wore green, ∴ Robinson wore green.

Other results follow simply: Smith was the Stoker and wore a red shirt; Brown was the Porter and wore a black shirt; Jones was the Guard and wore a blue shirt; Robinson was the Engine-driver and wore a green shirt.

3. Who Killed Popoff?

If A2 true, then B2 true, then A2 false. ∴ A2 false.

If B2 true then A and B have not made same number of true statements. ∴ B2 false. ∴ not everything that A says is false. ∴ A (and B) must have made at least 1 true statement.

If A3 true, then C2 true, then B1 false and B3 false, and A and B have not made same number of true statements. ∴ A3 false. ∴ A1 true (A must have made at least 1 true statement). ∴ C1 false.

If B3 true, then C2 false, then B1 true; but this is impossible as A and B must make same number of true statements. ∴ B3 false, ∴ B1 true and C2 false. ∴ C3 true (since B3 false).

But since A1 and B1 are both true, A and B must be innocent. ∴ Clarence killed Popoff (and some light is thrown on his third, carefully ambiguous remark).

4. Rithmetic Road

Their remarks, using obvious abbreviations, were:

A. Number of B's house is even.

B. (i) Number of my house > number of D's.
 (ii) My age is a perfect cube.

C. (i) Number of my house is 3 greater than number of A's.
 (ii) D's age is a multiple of A's age.

D. (i) B's age is either 27 or an even number other than 64.
 (ii) C does not live at number 19.

Since difference between age and house number is always 7, ∴ if house number is even, age is odd; and if house number is odd, age is even. ∴ false remarks made by those with odd ages and even houses; true remarks made by those with even ages and odd houses.

If B (ii) true B's age is 27 or 64, but if age is 27 remark is false, ∴ either B's age is 64 (and remark true), or B's age is an odd number other than 27 (and remark false). D (i) contradicts this, ∴ *D (i) false.*

∴ D's age is odd and his house number even; and *D(ii) is false.*

∴ *C lives at number 19; and C's age is 26* (it cannot be 19 – 7).

∴ C's remarks are true and from C (i) *A's house is 16.*

∴ *A's age is 23* (it cannot be 16 – 7).

∴ A's *remark is false.*

∴ B's house number is odd and B's age even.

But we know that B's age is either 64 or an odd number other than 27.

∴ *B's age is 64;*

∴ *B's remarks are true.*

Since C (ii) is true D's age is a multiple of 23.

But D's age is odd (see above). ∴ *D's age is 69.*

B (i) is true. ∴ number of B's house > number of D's.

But B's age < D's. ∴ B's house must be 64 + 7 (71) and D's house must be 69 – 7 (62).

∴ Complete solution is:

Alf is 23	and	lives	at	number	16
Bert is 64	,,	,,	,,	,,	71
Charlie is 26	,,	,,	,,	,,	19
Duggie is 69	,,	,,	,,	,,	62

5. The Cricket Dinner

It is easiest to set the facts out in a diagram thus. The five fellow members who made remarks are denoted by A, B, C, D, E in that order:

Date	A	B	C	D	E	*Date*	A	B	C	D	E
1	√	—	—	√	√	16	—	√	—	—	√
2	—	—	√	—	√	17	√	√	√	—	—
3	√	—	√	—	√	18	—	√	√	—	—
4	—	—	—	—	√	19	√	√	√	—	—
5	√	—	√	—	√	20	—	√	√	—	—
6	—	—	√	—	√	21	√	√	√	—	—
7	√	—	√	—	√	22	—	√	√	—	—
8	—	—	√	√	√	23	√	√	√	—	—
9	√	—	—	—	√	24	—	√	√	—	—
10	—	—	√	—	√	25	√	√	—	—	—
11	√	—	√	—	√	26	—	√	√	—	—
12	—	—	√	—	√	27	√	√	√	√	—
13	√	—	√	—	√	28	—	√	√	—	—
14	—	√	√	—	√	29	√	√	√	—	—
15	√	√	√	—	√	30	—	√	√	—	—
						31	√	√	√	—	—

√s below A denote the dates on which the dinner could have been if A's remark was true, —s denote the days on which it could have been if A's remark was false. Similarly for B, C, D, E.

The only date for which there is only one true remark is the 4th. This is therefore the date of the dinner.

6. On the Tiles

A diagram may help.

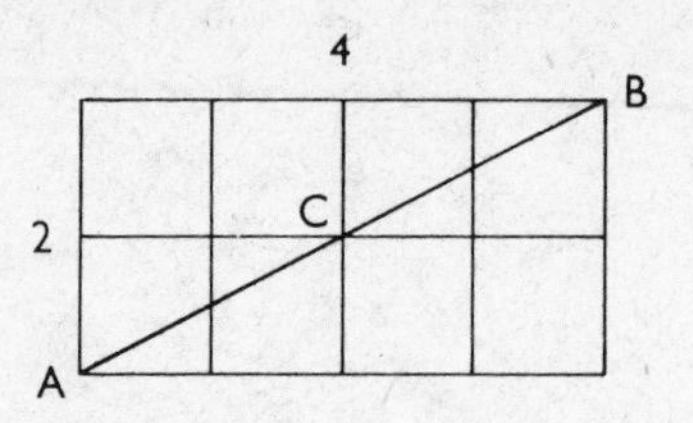

In going from A to B the line crosses 4 vertical lines and 2 horizontal lines (in both cases including line at B and excluding line at A). Every time it crosses a vertical or a horizontal line it has just passed through a square, but when it crosses a horizontal and a vertical line at the same time (as at C and B) it has just passed through one square and not two. Answer will therefore be: (number of vertical lines crossed) + (number of horizontal lines crossed) − (number of occasions when a vertical and horizontal line are crossed at the same time). This last bracket will be the Highest Common Factor of the numbers of vertical and horizontal lines — i.e. of the numbers of vertical and horizontal squares. ∴ in our diagram the answer is $(2+4-2)=4$.

In the first question given, since the H.C.F. of 81 and 63 is 9, the answer is $(81+63-9)=135$.

And since the H.C.F. of 472 and 296 is 8, ∴ the answer to the second question is $(472+296-8)=760$.

7. Homes, Houses and Hopes

1. Brewer not Cyril, not Cheltenham, ∴ C house (he must have one C).

2. If Cyril Dr, then Cyril Brazil (we know not Australia, and since Dr, ∴ not Dalmatia). ∴ Dr is Brazil; but we are told Dr not Brazil, ∴ Cyril not Dr, ∴ Cyril Author.

3. The Brewer not from Australia, not from Cheltenham, ∴ Brewer from Dalmatia.

4. Brewer from C house and from Dalmatia, ∴ Brewer must be Adolphus.

5. ∴ Dr not Adolphus, and Dr not Cyril, ∴ Dr is Basil and Desmond must be card-sharper.

6. Dr is Basil, ∴ not from B house ∴ Dr is from A house (only alternative left). ∴ Dr from Cheltenham.

7. Card-sharper is Desmond ∴ not from D house, ∴ from B house. ∴ Card-sharper from Australia.

8. ∴ Cyril, the Author, is from Brazil and was in D house.

Complete solution:

	Hopes	*Houses*	*Homes*
Adolphus	Brewer	C	Dalmatia
Basil	Doctor	A	Cheltenham
Cyril	Author	D	Brazil
Desmond	Card-sharper	B	Australia

8. Vests and Vocations

A diagram will help:

	baker	car- penter	hunter	walker	brown	cerise	helio- trope	white
Mr Baker	×				×			
Mr Carpenter	√	×	×	×		×		
Mr Hunter	×		×	×			×	
Mr Walker	×			×				×
brown	×		×					
cerise		×						
heliotrope			×					
white				×				

1. Mark in, as shown, the facts that Mr Baker is not the baker and does not wear a brown shirt, etc.

2. Mark in also, as shown, the facts given that Mr Hunter is not the walker, that the hunter did not wear a brown shirt, and that Mr Carpenter was the baker. (Note that from this last, positive, information we can deduce, as shown, that Mr Carpenter is not the hunter or the walker, and that the baker is not Mr Hunter, or Mr Walker.)

(These facts are marked in. The reader is advised to mark in other facts as they are discovered.)

3. By elimination Mr Baker was the walker. ∴ by elimination Mr Walker was the hunter. ∴ by elimination Mr Hunter was the carpenter.

4. Since the walker was Mr Baker, who did not wear a brown shirt, ∴ the walker did not wear a brown shirt. Similarly Mr Baker did not wear a white shirt. By elimination the carpenter wore a brown shirt. ∴ Mr Hunter (who is the carpenter) wore a brown shirt.

5. ∴ by elimination Mr Carpenter wore a white shirt. ∴ the baker (Mr Carpenter) wore a white shirt.

6. ∴ by elimination the hunter wore a cerise shirt and by elimination the walker wore a heliotrope shirt, and rest follows easily.

∴ complete solution is:
Mr Baker is the walker and wore a heliotrope shirt; Mr Carpenter is the baker and wore a white shirt; Mr Hunter is the carpenter and wore a brown shirt; Mr Walker is the hunter and wore a cerise shirt.

9. Ping Pong Pill Passes on

Trace the movements of each.

SMITH: A at 9.14; E at 9.52. Could not have caught train from B to E (it didn't arrive until 9.53). ∴ cycled (28 minutes), leaving B not later than 9.24. ∴ *not guilty and did not leave bicycle.* (He must have caught 9.15 from A, arriving at B at 9.23.)

BROWN: E at 9.1; C at 9.58. Bicycled E to B, arriving not earlier than 9.29. ∴ *not guilty.* Has missed 9.25 to C. ∴ cycled on, arriving between 9.57 and 9.58. *Did not leave bicycle.*

JONES: A at 9.14 (seen by Smith); D at 10.9 (left bicycle at A). ∴ caught 9.15 from A to B; and 9.25 from B to D. ∴ *not guilty. Bicycle at B not his.*

ROBINSON: C at 8.56; D at 10.3 (must have left bicycle at B). Train from B to D at 9.25 ∴ *not guilty.* Bicycled from C to B (28 minutes), arriving B 9.24–9.25.

GREEN: E at 8.59; A at 9.40. (must have left bicycle at B). ∴ caught 9.30 from B to A. Could not have caught 8.58 from E, ∴ bicycled from E to B (28 minutes). ∴ could have been in B at *9.27.* ∴ he had from *9.27 to 9.30* in which to commit murder. ∴ Bicycles belonged to Robinson and Green.

Green was the murderer.

10. Liars Again

Suppose S3 is true, so that all R's statements are true.

Since R1 is true, ∴ J2 is false.

Since R2 is true, ∴ J3 is false.

Since R4 is true, ∴ J1 and J4 are true.

Since J4 is true, ∴ S3 is false.

But this is contrary to hypothesis. ∴ S3 cannot be true. ∴ not all R's statements are true, and not all S's statements are true (S3 false).

∴ *all J's statements must be true* (one person made 4 true statements.)

∴ from J4 *all S's statements are untrue,* and from looking at R's statements we see that they too are all false.

11. The Poison Spreads

Diagrams will help.

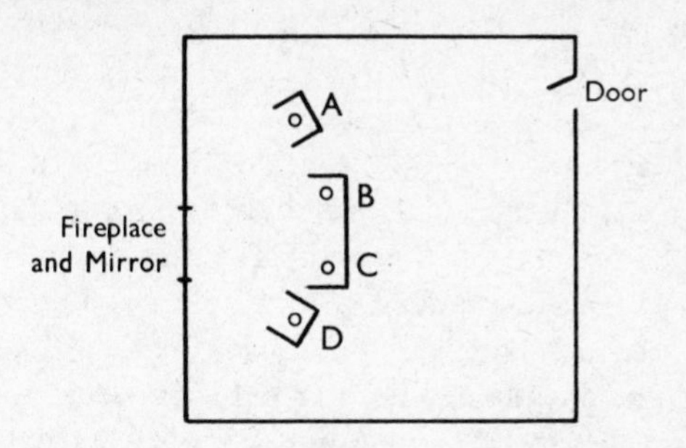

	General	Schoolmaster	Admiral	Doctor
Smith				
Brown		×		
Jones		×		
Robinson	×			

1. From (i) and (iv) Schoolmaster not Jones or Brown (mark in diagram as shown).

2. From (ii) General not Robinson (mark in diagram). And General must be C or D (see first diagram) to see door in mirror. Robinson not A.

3. From (v) Smith not Admiral or Schoolmaster. ∴ by elimination *Robinson is Schoolmaster*.

4. Also from (v) *Smith sitting at A; Schoolmaster at B*.

5. Since General next to Robinson (ii) and sitting at C or D. ∴ *General at C*. ∴ General not Smith. ∴ by elimination *Smith is the Doctor*. ∴ by elimination *Admiral sitting at D*.

6. Since Smith is Admiral's brother-in-law and neither Smith nor Brown has got any sisters, ∴ Admiral not Brown. ∴ *Brown is General*, and *Jones is Admiral*.

A, Dr Smith; B, Schoolmaster Robinson; C, General Brown; D, Admiral Jones.

The hand putting something into Jones's whisky must belong to *General Brown*.

12. The Mathematics Paper

(i) Total for (2) = 29. ∴ 17 cannot be right answer (this would result in 3 10s).

Total can only be $2 \times 10 + 7 + 2 + 0$. ∴ 43 is right answer (10 marks) and A must have got 43.

(ii) Total for (4) = 42. This can only be $4 \times 10 + 2$. E only got 9 marks altogether, ∴ E did not get (4) right, ∴ everybody else did, ∴ right answer is 6*s* and E got 2 marks.

(iii) B got 10 marks for (4) and only 19 altogether ∴ all other answers wrong. ∴ 5 is not answer to (3).

(iv) Total for (3) = 22. This can only be $2 \times 10 + 2$. ∴ 11 must be right answer to (3), and A and D each got 10 marks for it.

(v) C's total is 31, and C got 10 marks for (2) and 10 for (4). 31 must be made up of $10 + 10 + 7 + 2 + 2$. ∴ C's answer to (1) is wrong. And answers of A, B, and E to (1) are wrong (the 10 marks for the right answer would give them too many). ∴ D's answer to (1) (2′ 6″) must be right, and he gets 10 marks for it.

(vi) Similarly only D can have the right answer to (5) (3·8; 10 marks).

(vii) A's total of 34 must be $3 \times 10 + 2 \times 2$. ∴ A's answers to (1) and (5) must receive 2 marks each.

(viii) C (1) must get 7 or 2 (see(v)). But not 7, because total for (1) is 14 ($10 + 2 + 2$). ∴ C (1) gets 2. ∴ B (1) and E (1) each get 0.

(ix) C (3) must get 7 or 2 (see above). But since total for (3) is 22, and A and B get 10 each, ∴ C (3) gets 2. ∴ B (3) and E (3) each get 0, and C (5) gets 7 (total for C is 31).

(x) E got 2 for (4) and 9 altogether, ∴ 7 for one other question. We are told that E got more marks for (5) than B did. ∴ E got 7 for (5) and B must have got 2 or 0.

(xi) B got 9 for (2) and (5) between them, ∴ 7 for (2) and 2 for (5).

(xii) E got 0 for (2), and since there were altogether 29 for (2), D must have got 2.

Complete answers and marks (in brackets) are therefore:

	1		2		3		4		5		Total marks
A	5′	(2)	43	(10)	11	(10)	6*s*.	(10)	4·5	(2)	(34)
B	3′ 6″	(0)	17	(7)	5	(0)	6*s*.	(10)	3·4	(2)	(19)
C	4′	(2)	43	(10)	5	(2)	6*s*.	(10)	2·8	(7)	(31)
D	2′ 6″	(10)	17	(2)	11	(10)	6*s*.	(10)	3·8	(10)	(42)
E	7′	(0)	17	(0)	7	(0)	7*s*.	(2)	5·2	(7)	(9)
Total marks for different questions		(14)		(29)		(22)		(42)		(28)	(135)

13. Abacus Avenue

(i) Consider C (1). If true, this number can only be 64, in this case all C's statements are false. This is impossible. ∴ statement false, and C's number > 50, but not 64.

(ii) ∴ C (2) false. ∴ D's statements true.

(iii) From D (1) D's number must be 16, 25, 36 or 49.

(iv) D (2) true. ∴ B (1) false (there is no cube between 70 and 111). ∴ B's number a cube between 50 and 70, ∴ 64.

(v) B (2) false. ∴ A's number not more than 30. ∴ A truthful, and from A (1) A's number can only be 16.

(vi) E (1) cannot be true (highest number is 111). ∴ E's number > 50.

(vii) A (2) true. We know that D is 16, 25, 36 or 49 (see (iii)) and E > 50. ∴ D must be 49 and E 59.

(viii) C must live in same house as one of the others, and since C is a liar it must be B or E. From (i) we know that C does not live in 64, where B lives. ∴ C lives in same house as E, 59.

∴ numbers are: A = 16; B = 64; C = 59; D = 49; E = 59.

14.

(i) B cannot have lost a match (no goals scored against them). ∴ A *v.* B not a win. But A won one ∴ A beat C.

(ii) ∴ C lost to A and their drawn match must have been against B. Score in drawn match (C *v.* B) must have been 0–0 (no goals scored against B). ∴ Score in B's other match must have been 3–0. ∴ B *v.* A was 3–0.

(iii) As A scored no goals *v.* B, they must have scored all their goals (4) *v.* C. C scored no goals *v.* B, ∴ C scored all their goals (2) *v.* A.

∴ A *v.* B was 0–3; A *v.* C was 4–2; B *v.* C was 0–0.

15. Fill up figures in table given and in the following table as they are discovered.

	A	B	C	D
A	X		*d* 3–3	–0
B		X		–0
C	*d* 3–3		X	–0
D	0–	0–	0–	X

(i) Fill up, as shown, fact that C *v.* A was 3–3 and that D scored no goals. (Other facts should be filled in as discovered).

(ii) A had 5 goals scored against them, 3 by C, 0 by D, and therefore 2 by B.

(iii) Since B won all three matches ∴ B *v.* A was 2–0 or 2–1.

(iv) D scored no goals and drew one match. ∴ score in drawn match was 0–0 and scores in other two matches were 0–1 and 0–2 (only 3 goals against).

(v) A scored not more than 1 goal against B (see (iii)), and not more than 2 against D (see (iv)). But A scored 3 against C and more than 5 altogether ∴ 1 against B and 2 against D.

(vi) Since B scôred 4 goals altogether, including 2 against A, and won all three matches, ∴ B *v.* C and B *v.* D must each have been 1–0.

(vii) D had 3 goals scored against them; 2 by A and 1 by B. ∴ 0 by C. ∴ D *v.* C was 0–0.

Complete table of results is therefore:

	A	B	C	D
A	X	*l* 1–2	*d* 3–3	*w* 2–0
B	*w* 2–1	X	*w* 1–0	*w* 1–0
C	*d* 3–3	*l* 0–1	X	*d* 0–0
D	*l* 0–2	*l* 0–1	*d* 0–0	X

16.

(i) D must have played at least 1 match (1 drawn, etc); and not more than 3. But total of matches played must be *even* (each match occurs twice). ∴ D played 2.

(ii) A *v.* B was 3–1, ∴ A's other match was lost 0–2. (A's totals of goals 3–3).

(iii) D drew one. And since D's totals of goals were 4–7, D lost other match by 3 goals. ∴ D did not play A. ∴ A's other match (0–2) was *v.* C.

(iv) A drew no matches and C could not have drawn more than 1 (C beat A). But total of drawn matches in table must be even (each match occurs twice). ∴ C drew none. ∴ B *v.* D was a draw, and this was only drawn match.

(v) Since B played A and D, B did not play C. ∴ C's other match was *v.* D.

Conclusions reached so far can be shown in a table, thus:

	A	B	C	D
A	X	*w* 3–1	*l* 0–2	X
B	*l* 1–3	X	X	*d*
C	*w* 2–0	X	X	
D	X	*d*		X

(vi) B scored 4 goals altogether, 1 *v.* A, ∴ 3 *v.* D. But B *v.* D was a draw, ∴ score was 3–3.

(vii) Since D's totals of goals were 4–7 ∴ score in D's other match (*v.* C) must have been 1–4.

∴ Scores were: A *v.* B = 3–1; B *v.* D = 3–3; A *v.* C = 0–2; C *v.* D = 4–1.

17.

From what K says A's 'goals for' are such that if we know them we can deduce everything. A's 'goals for' must be at least 2. (A won both matches). If more than 2, we would have no way of knowing how many A scored against B, how many against C, and whether any goals were scored against A.

∴ A's goals for must be 2.

∴ A *v.* B was 1–0, and A *v.* C was 1–0.

And since C scored 3 goals (none against A) and drew against B, ∴ B *v.* C was 3–3.

∴ A *v.* B = 1–0; A *v.* C = 1–0; B *v.* C = 3–3.

18.

It will be helpful to copy the table given and to fill in the missing figures as found.

A table giving complete results will also be helpful.

	A	B	C	D	E
A	X				*w* 1–0
B		X	–3		
C		3–	X		
D				X	
E	*l* 0–1				X

(i) Fill in, as shown, the fact that C scored 3 goals against B.

(ii) Since A's goals are 3–1 for 4 matches, none of which were drawn, A must have won 3 matches by 1–0 and lost the other 0–1, but we don't yet know which match A lost.

(iii) Since E scored only 1 pt., E drew one and lost the rest. ∴ A beat E 1–0 (A played everyone and drew none).

(Fill in this result in table, as shown. Other results should be filled in, as found).

(iv) Total of draws so far is 5 (C2, D2, E1). ∴ B drew 1 or 3 (total must be even, since each draw appears twice). But B *v.* A not a draw (A drew none) ∴ B drew 1.

∴ C *v.* D a draw. (C and D must each have drawn against either B or E; their other drawn match must have been against each other).

(v) E drew 1 match and won none. They had 4 goals for and 5 against. ∴ they can only have lost one match. ∴ they only played two (one against A, 0–1; the other they must have drawn 4–4). E's drawn match must have been against C or D (see (iv)). But D only had 3 goals for and 2 against. ∴ E's draw was against C (4–4).

(vi) Total of matches played must be even (each one appears twice). So far it is $4+3+4+2=13$. ∴ D must have played

1 or 3. But we know that D drew 2, ∴ D played 3. ∴ the only teams that did not play against each other were B and E, and D and E.

(vii) D drew against C and ∴ drew one other match. D *v.* A *not* a draw (A drew none) ∴ D *v.* B a draw.

(viii) ∴ D must have beaten A (D got 4 pts.) and score must have been 1–0. And A *v.* B and A *v.* C must both have been 1–0 (See (ii)).

(ix) ∴ A scored 1 goal against B. C scored 3 goals against B (given), ∴ D scored 0 goals against B (total 4). But B *v.* D was a draw, ∴ score was 0–0.

(x) B scored 4 goals, 0 against A and 0 against D ∴ B scored 4 against C and score was 4–3.

(xi) D *v.* A was 1–0, D *v.* B was 0–0, ∴ D *v.* C was 2–2 (D's totals of goals were 3–2).

Complete table of results is therefore:

	A	B	C	D	E
A	X	*w* 1–0	*w* 1–0	*l* 0–1	*w* 1–0
B	*l* 0–1	X	*w* 4–3	*d* 0–0	X
C	*l* 0–1	*l* 3–4	X	*d* 2–2	*d* 4–4
D	*w* 1–0	*d* 0–0	*d* 2–2	X	X
E	*l* 0–1	X	*d* 4–4	X	X

19.

(i) Total of matches played must be even (each match appears twice). Total of A, C, D, E is 13; ∴ B must have played 1 or 3. But A and D each played everyone (4 matches). ∴ B played 3.

(ii) Total number of matches is 8 ($16 \div 2$). ∴ total points = 16. ∴ B got 5 pts [$16 - (5 + 3 + 3)$].

(iii) C played 3, lost 0 and got 3 pts. ∴ C must have drawn 3. ∴ goals for = goals against = 4.

(iv) Total of goals for = total of goals against. ∴ D had 10 goals against.

A diagram will help, in which information can be filled in as found.

	A	B	C	D	E
A	X		*d*		
B		X	*d*		X
C	*d*	*d*	X	*d*	X
D			*d*	X	
E		X	X		X

(v) C drew 3 (see (iii)). Not against E who got no points. ∴ C drew *v.* A, B and D and did not play E. (These facts have been marked in diagram.)

(vi) Since A and D played everyone, B was the other side that did not play E.

(This has also been marked in diagram. The reader may like to insert other information in his own diagram as it is found).

(vii) E lost both their matches, *v.* A and D. D beat E and drew *v.* C, but only got 3 pts. altogether. ∴ D lost to A and to B.

(viii) A beat D and E and drew *v.* C, but only got 5 pts. ∴ A lost to B.

(We now know who played whom, and the result of each match).

(ix) A lost to B, but only had 1 goal scored against. ∴ A *v.* B was 0–1.

(x) ∴ no one else scored against A. ∴ A *v.* C (a draw) was 0–0. A *v.* D and A *v.* E were both ?–0.

(xi) E scored 2 goals; 0 *v.* A, ∴ 2 *v.* D.

(xii) ∴ D scored at least 3 *v.* E (to win). ∴ D scored not more than 2 *v.* C (D's total 5). ∴ D *v.* C not more than 2–2. ∴ B *v.* C not less than 2–2 (C's totals: 4–4). But B only had 2 goals scored against them. ∴ B *v.* C not more than 2–2. ∴ B *v.* C was 2–2.

(xiii) ∴ C's remaining match (*v.* D) was 2–2.

(xiv) From B's total of goals for and against B *v.* D was 2–0.

(xv) Total against D 10 (2 by B, 2 by C, 2 by E). ∴ 4 by A. ∴ D *v.* A was 0–4.

(xvi) From A's totals of goals, A *v.* E was 3–0.

(xvii) From E's total of goals against, E *v.* D was 2–3.

Summary of results:

	A	B	C	D	E
A	X	*l* 0–1	*d* 0–0	*w* 4–0	*w* 3–0
B	*w* 1–0	X	*d* 2–2	*w* 2–0	X
C	*d* 0–0	*d* 2–2	X	*d* 2–2	X
D	*l* 0–4	*l* 0–2	*d* 2–2	X	*w* 3–2
E	*l* 0–3	X	X	*l* 2–3	X

20.

Table in which information can be inserted as discovered:

	A	B	C	D	E
A	X		*d*		
B		X	*d*	X	
C	*d*	*d*	X	*d*	X
D		X	*d*	X	X
E			X	X	X

(i) Total number of matches is 7 [(4 + 3 + 3 + 2 + 2) ÷ 2]. ∴ total points is 14. ∴ B obtained 5 points.

(ii) C obtained 3 points and won no matches. ∴ 3 draws. ∴ 5 goals for.

(iii) D obtained 1 pt, ∴ drew 1 and lost 1. E obtained 0 pt, ∴ lost 2.

(iv) C drew 3 matches — not against E (who lost 2), ∴ against A, B, D, and C did not play E.

(v) A played all the others (4 matches). ∴ D played against A and C, but no one else (only 2 matches), and E played against A and B, but no one else.

(We now have complete information about who played whom, and we know which matches were drawn. This information has been inserted in the table. The reader may like to put in other information as it is obtained.)

(vi) Since E won none, E *v.* A and E *v.* B were lost, and since D drew 1 and lost 1, D *v.* A was lost.

(vii) A scored 5 points (1 *v.* C, 2 *v.* D, and 2 *v.* E). ∴ A lost to B.

(We now know the results of all the matches.)

(viii) E scored no goals in either of their matches.

(ix) A lost 1 match (*v.* B), but only had 1 goal scored against them. ∴ A *v.* B was 0–1.

(x) B had no goals scored against them by A or E, but 2 goals against them altogether. ∴ 2 by C. But B *v.* C a draw,

∴ score 2–2, ∴ B scored 4 against E (7 – 2 – 1), ∴ E *v.* A was 0–1 (E's totals 0–5).

(xi) A only had 1 goal scored against them (by B). ∴ A's draw *v.* C was 0–0. ∴ score in A's remaining match (*v.* D) was 7–0.

(xii) C's total was 5–5 (0–0 *v.* A, 2–2 *v.* B). ∴ 3–3 *v.* D.

∴ complete table of results is:

	A	B	C	D	E
A	X	*l* 0–1	*d* 0–0	*w* 7–0	*w* 1–0
B	*w* 1–0	X	*d* 2–2	X	*w* 4–0
C	*d* 0–0	*d* 2–2	X	*d* 3–3	X
D	*l* 0–7	X	*d* 3–3	X	X
E	*l* 0–1	*l* 0–4	X	X	X

21.

Diagrams will help.

1.

	Played	*Won*	*Lost*	*Drawn*	*Goals for*	*Goals against*	*Points*
C	4		1		7		6
A	4					7	
E	4			1	9		5
B	4			3		3	
D	4					3	1

2.

	C	A	E	B	D
C	X	*l* −4	*w*	*w*	*w*
A	*w* 4−	X	*l* −5	*d*	*w*
E	*l*	*w* 5−	X	*d* 2−	*w*
B	*l*	*d*	*d* −2	X	*d*
D	*l*	*l*	*l*	*d*	X

The first diagram has been left as given. In the second diagram the facts given have been inserted and the results, but not the scores, as found in the following arguments. The reader is recommended to fill up his own diagram with the facts as found.

(i) D only 1 pt. ∴ drew 1 and lost 3.

(ii) C got 6 pts. and lost 1 match. ∴ won 3, drew none.

(iii) B drew 3, but not *v.* C. ∴ *v.* A, E and D. ∴ A drew one.

(iv) D drew *v.* B, ∴ lost to C, A and E.

(v) A drew one and ∴ got odd number of points. Not 7 as A below C, ∴ 5. ∴ A won 2 and lost 1.

(vi) E drew one and got 5 pts. ∴ E won 2 and lost 1.

(vii) To make total of matches lost equal to total of matches won, B must have lost fourth match (*v.* C).

(The first table is now completed except for the goals.)

(viii) We are told that A did not score as many as 4 goals except *v.* C. ∴ A *v.* E lost. ∴ E's remaining match (*v.* C.) was lost, and C's remaining match *v.* A was lost.

(We now know result of every match, as shown in diagram (2)).

(ix) E *v.* B a draw ∴ score 2–2. (E scored 2 goals *v.* B.)

(x) B's goals for must be less than goals against (3*d*, 1*l*). Total against 3, and B scored 2 *v.* E ∴ B *v.* A and B *v.* D were both 0–0, and B *v.* C 0–1.

(xi) D lost 3 matches (*v.* C, A and E), but only had 3 goals scored against. ∴ score in each was 0–1.

(xii) E scored 9 goals (5 *v.* A, 2 *v.* B, 1 *v.* D) ∴ 1 *v.* C.

(xiii) A had 7 goals against (5 by E, 0 by B, 0 by D) ∴ 2 by C.

(xiv) C scored 7 goals (2 *v.* A, 1 *v.* B, 1 *v.* D) ∴ 3 *v.* E.

(xv) We still have to find how many goals A scored *v.* E. We know it is less than 4. And since A is above E with same number of points scored, A's goal average must be higher than E's. If A scored 2 *v.* E, A's average $= \frac{7}{7}$, and E's average $= \frac{9}{7}$. And E would be above A (obviously if A scored less than 2 *v.* E, E would be above A).

∴ A must have scored 3 *v.* E (A's average $= \frac{8}{7}$, E's average $= \frac{9}{8}$)

Results are: C *v.* A = 2–4; A *v.* E = 3–5; E *v.* B = 2–2; C *v.* E = 3–1; A *v.* B = 0–0; E *v.* D = 1–0; C *v.* B = 1–0; A *v.* D = 1–0; B *v.* D = 0–0; C *v.* D = 1–0.

22. Blots on the Evidence

We must think carefully about what must be in Alf's mind — remembering that he does not know, for example, that at least one goal was scored in each match. We know that B won all three matches.

∴ B beat D. D only had 1 goal against.

∴ B *v.* D must have been 1–0. And neither A nor C scored against D.

In the supplementary information we are told that B *v.* C was the same as D *v.* A. We know that D *v.* A was ? –0.

∴ B *v.* C must be ?–0.

In fact B *v.* C must be 1–0 as B wins each of their three matches by a single goal (goals for 5; goals against 2).

∴ D *v.* A is 1–0, and B *v.* A must be 3–2.

We now have:

	A	B	C	D
A	X	2–3		0–1
B	3–2		1–0	1–0
C		0–1	X	0–
D	1–0	0–1	–0	X

We are told that C drew 1 match.

∴ C *v.* A or C *v.* D was a draw. But not C *v.* D for at least one goal was scored in every match.

∴ C *v.* A must be a draw and since C had 4 goals for it must be 4–4. And since C had 8 goals against,

C *v.* D must be 0–3.

Complete results are therefore: A *v.* B = 2–3; B *v.* C = 1–0; A *v.* C = 4–4; B *v.* D = 1–0; A *v.* D = 0–1; C *v.* D = 0–3.

23. Muddle and Mess Once More

1.

	Played	*Won*	*Lost*	*Drawn*	*Goals for*	*Goals against*	*Points*
A	3				1		3
B	3				2	3	4
C	3			2		1	3
D	3			0			2
E	3				3	4	1

We must first discover which of these figures are wrong.

(i) Total of matches played should be even (each match appears twice). But it is 15. ∴ a mistake in the 'Played' column. Similarly total of points scored should be even (two points for each match). But it is 13. ∴ a mistake in the 'Points' column.

(ii) If C played 3, and drew 2, they must have won or lost one ∴ Points cannot be 3 ∴ a mistake in the C row. If E played 3 and scored 1 point, they must have lost two and drawn one. ∴ total of goals for must be more than one less than total of goals against. ∴ their goals cannot be 3–4. ∴ a mistake in the E row.

(iii) Since there are mistakes in the Played column and in the Points column, and mistakes in the C row and in the E row, but only two mistakes altogether, ∴ these mistakes must

2.

	A	B	C	D	E
A	X		*d*		
B		X	*l* 0–3		
C	*d*	*w* 3–0	X	X	*d*
D			X	X	
E			*d*		X

be in diagonally opposite corners of the rectangle formed by these lines. But no change in number of matches played by C will make their points 3, with 2 drawn matches. ∴ change must be in E's matches played and C's points scored.

If E's matches were 4 then C's points would have to be 6 to make total of points 16 for the 8 matches. But C drew 2 of their 3 matches and could not have scored 6 points.

∴ E's matches must be 2, and ∴ C's points 4 (to make total 14 for 7 matches.)

A table of results will help (see table 2).

(iv) If B had got their 4 points by 1 win and 2 draws, their goals for would be more than their goals against. But in fact their goals are 2–3 ∴ They must have won 2 and lost 1. And the scores can only have been 1–0, 1–0, and 0–3. ∴ B drew none, and C's 2 drawn matches must have been *v.* E (who only got 1 pt) and *v.* A (Insert in table, as shown, the fact that C drew against A and E.)

(v) We are told that C played B and this must therefore have been C's third match, which they won. B only lost one match (0–3). ∴ this was score in B *v.* C. And we know that since C played A, B, and E they did not play D. (Insert these facts in table as shown. The reader may like to insert other facts as they are discovered.)

(vi) ∴ D's matches were *v.* A, B and E. And since we now know that E only played 2 matches, these were against C and D, and E did not play against A or B. ∴ A's third match was *v.* B. And we know exactly who played whom.

(vii) B *v.* C is 0–3. And we know that scores in B's other two matches were 1–0, 1–0 (see (iv)) ∴ B *v.* A and B *v.* D were both 1–0.

(viii) A lost to B, drew with C and scored 3 pts. ∴ A *v.* D was a win. And since A only scored 1 goal A *v.* D was 1–0. And A's drawn match (*v.* C) must have been 0–0.

(ix) C had one goal scored against them. Not by A and not by B, ∴ by E. But C *v.* E was a draw ∴ score was 1–1.

(x) E's total goals were 3–4. 1–1 *v.* C, ∴ 2–3 *v.* D.

We now know score in every match.

	A	B	C	D	E
A	X	0–1	0–0	1–0	X
B	1–0	X	0–3	1–0	X
C	0–0	3–0	X	X	1–1
D	0–1	0–1	X	X	3–2
E	X	X	1–1	2–3	X

24. Uncle Claudius Again

A diagram in which results and scores can be filled in as they are found will be helpful. Thus:

	A	B	C	D
A	X			*w* –0
B		X	–2	*w* –0
C		2–	X	*w* –0
D	*l* 0–	*l* 0–	*l* 0–	X

(i) Total of goals for (16) is different from total of goals against (17), ∴ there is a mistake in one of these columns.

(ii) C drew 2 matches, and must have won or lost the other. ∴ C's goals for cannot be equal to C's goals against. ∴ either C's 4 goals for or 4 goals against must be wrong. All other figures right.

(iii) D scored no goals and got no points. ∴ all 3 matches lost (0–?). (This information has been inserted in the diagram. Other information should be added as found.)

(iv) C did not draw against D. ∴ drew against A and B, and beat D (4 pts). ∴ score in C *v*. B was 2–2.

(v) Since A scored 5 pts and drew against C, ∴ A beat B as well as D. We now know the result of every match and have only to discover the scores and the mistake in C's goals for or against.

(vi) B's total of goals against is 3. 2 of these were scored by C, 0 by D, ∴ 1 goal scored by A, and as B lost to A score was 0–1.

(vii) ∴ from total of goals, B *v*. D was 3–0.

(viii) A had 1 goal scored against — not by B or D, ∴ by C. A *v*. C was a draw ∴ score 1–1.

(ix) ∴ C only had 3 goals scored against, ∴ this is the

mistake. C's goals against should be 3 instead of 4, and since C scored 4 goals ∴ C *v.* D was 1–0.

(x) Since A's total of goals for was 7 ∴ A *v.* D was 5–0.

Final diagram giving results and scores is therefore:

	A	B	C	D
A	X	*w* 1–0	*d* 1–1	*w* 5–0
B	*l* 0–1	X	*d* 2–2	*w* 3–0
C	*d* 1–1	*d* 2–2	X	*w* 1–0
D	*l* 0–5	*l* 0–3	*l* 0–1	X

25. Hitler and Goering

H I T L E R	– – – – – –
G O E R I N G	– – – – – – –
H T T L L H H H	– – – – – – – –

Important to have a pattern, as above, and to fill in the blanks as they are found.

(i) When two numbers are added together, the most that can be carried is 1. ∴ H = 1. (Fill in 1 wherever H occurs.)

(ii) Since the most that can be carried is 1, G must be 9, and T must be 0.

(iii) ∴ H + O (and perhaps 1 carried from I + E) = 10. O cannot be 9 (G is 9), ∴ O must be 8 and there *is* 1 carried from I + E.

(iv) Look now at the other end. G = 9, H = 1, ∴ R = 2.

(v) Fill in 2 for the other R (below T) and we have 0 + 2 apparently producing L. But L cannot be 2, ∴ there must have been 1 to carry (from L + I) and L = 3.

(vi) Below L + I (3 + ?) we have H (1). I cannot be 8 (O = 8) ∴ I = 7 and there was 1 to carry from E + N.

(vii) Look now at the E of G O E R I N G, and it is easy to see that it must be 6. ∴ N = 4. Complete solution is:

$$
\begin{array}{r}
170362 \\
9862749 \\
\hline
10033111 \\
\hline
\end{array}
$$

26.

```
        ______________________________
- - - ) - - - - - - 5 - - - 8
        - - -
        _____
              - - - 5               a
                - - -               b
                _____
                    - - - -         c
                    - - - -
                    _______
                          - - 8 o d
                          - - 8 o
                          _______

                          _______
```

(i) Fill in 5 and 8, as shown, where they will be brought down, and fill in figure to the right of 8 in *d* (it must be 0).

(ii) Since *b* subtracted from *a* produces a number less than ten, ∴ *a* must be 1005 and *b* greater than 995.

(iii) Since a multiple of *b* or a multiple of a factor of *b* ends in 0 (see *d*), and since *b* cannot end in 5 or 0 ∴ *b* must end with an even digit. ∴ *b* is 996 or 998.

(iv) ∴ *c* is either 9 – – – or 7 – – –, ∴ divisor is greater than 700 (otherwise last figure in *c* would not have been brought down). ∴ divisor is 996 or 998.

(v) *d* is 5 times divisor. ∴ divisor is 996 ($5 \times 996 = 4980$; $5 \times 998 = 4990$). ∴ *d* is 4980.

(vi) *c* must start with 9. ∴ 4 figure number below *c* is 8964 (996×9).

Rest follows easily.

```
         10010090·5
    ──────────────
996)9970050138
    996
    ───
      1005
       996
      ────
         9013
         8964
         ────
           4980
           4980
           ────

           ────
```

27.

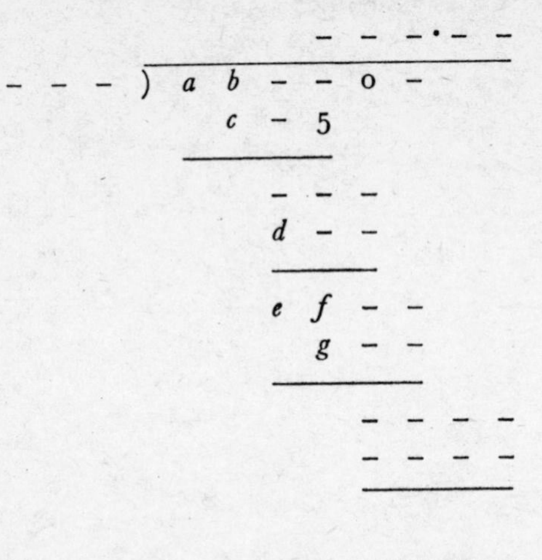

(i) c must be 9, and $a\ b$ must be 10.

(ii) d cannot be 9; if it were there would be no figure immediately below it. ∴ divisor is not 9 – 5, but is a factor of 9 – 5.

(iii) Last two figures in last two rows must be 00 ∴ divisor goes exactly into – – 0 0. And since we know that divisor is a factor of 9 – 5 it does not end in 0. It is easy to see that it must end in 25 or 75; and since it goes exactly into 9 – 5 it can only be 325.

(iv) g must be 9, and $e\,f$ must be 10.

(v) ∴ number starting g must be 975.

(vi) The last division (325 into – – 0 0) must either be 4×325 (1300) or 8×325 (2600). If the former, line $e\ f$ – – would be less than 1000 ($975 + 13$). ∴ last division must be 8×325 (2600), and rest follows easily.

```
       323·08
325)105001
    975
    ---
     750
     650
     ---
     1001
      975
     ----
       2600
       2600
       ----
```

28.

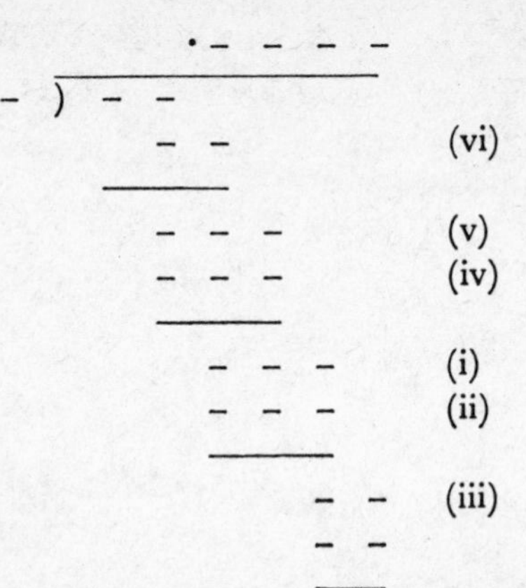

1. Since there are only two figures in dividend each figure brought down must be 0, and the quotient must consist of a decimal point followed by four figures. ∴ 3rd figure of (i) is 0. ∴ 3rd figure of (ii) is not 0 (if it were, (iii) would be 0 0, which would be absurd). ∴ divisor does not end in 0 (if it did, every multiple of it would end in 0.)

2. If divisor ends in 5, (iii) must be 50, and divisor must be 25. First subtraction would then have to be 75 from – – 0, which is impossible, for divisor would have gone four times, producing three figures. ∴ divisor does not end in 5.

3. ∴ in last division divisor must go 5 times (to end in 0), into a number less than 100. ∴ divisor less than 20, and must be 12, 14, 16 or 18.

If 14, (iii) would be 70 (5×14) and (ii) would end in 3, which is impossible for a multiple of 14.

If 18, (iii) would be 90 and (ii) would end in 1; — impossible.

If 12, (iii) would be 60 and (ii) would end in 4. But (ii) is 12 multiplied by a figure less than 10; it cannot therefore end in 4. ($12 \times 9 = 108$). ∴ Divisor must be 16.

4. ∴ (iii) is 80, and (ii) ends in 2. ∴ (ii) must be 112 (16×7) and (i) must be 120 ($112 + 8$).

5. ∴ (iv) must be 16 multiplied by less than 10, ending in 8. It can only be 16 × 8 (128). (16 × 3 ends in 8, but only has 2 figures.)

6. ∴ (v) is 140 (128 + 12), and (vi) must clearly be the largest two-figure multiple of 16 (96).

Complete solution:

```
      ·6875
   ────────
16)11·0
   9 6
   ───
   1 40
   1 28
   ────
     120
     112
     ───
      80
      80
      ──
```

29.

```
              _ _ _._ _
        ___________________
  _ _ ) 1 0 _ _ _
        9 _
        ___
          a a
          _ _
          ___
          _ 3 _           (v)
          _ _ _           (iv)
          _____
              _ 0         (i)
              _ b         (ii)
              ___
                _ 0       (iii)
                _ _
                ___
```

1. When there are no more figures to bring down a decimal point is put in the answer and 0s are brought down, as shown.

2. Since, in the first subtraction, the result of subtracting 2 figures from 3 figures is to produce one figure, ∴ 9 – must be subtracted from 10 – (as shown.)

3. Divisor cannot end in 0, for if it did *b* would be 0 which would be absurd (next line would be 00.)

4. Divisor cannot be 9 –, for greatest value of (i) is 90, and (ii) would then be greater than (i).

5. If *b* were 5, last division would be into 50 and divisor could only be 25. But 25 does not go exactly into 9 –, ∴ divisor does not end in 5. ∴ Since bottom line ends in 0, divisor must be multiplied by 5; and since bottom line only has two figures, ∴ divisor must be less than 20. 12, 14, 16, 18 are only possibilities (to go exactly into – 0.)

6. If divisor were 14, (iii) would be 70 and *b* 3, which is impossible. If divisor were 18, (iii) would be 90 and *b* 1, which is impossible.

7. If divisor were 12 the greatest possible value of (iv) would be 108 (12×9) and this subtracted from – 3 – must leave more than a single figure. ∴ divisor is 16.

8. ∴ (iii) is 80, ∴ *b* is 2 and (ii) is 32. ∴ (i) is 40, (iv) must be 128 and (v) 132.

9. The multiple of 16 which subtracted from *a a* leaves 13 can only be 64, and $a = 7$. The rest follows easily and final solution is:

```
      648·25
   ---------
16)10372
    96
    --
    77
    64
    --
    132
    128
    ---
     40
     32
     --
      80
      80
      --
```

30.

(i) Consider first division. 3 figures subtracted from 4 figures leaves 1 figure. ∴ divisor must go exactly into something between 991 and 999.

(ii) But from second division we see that remainder from first division is 1. ∴ divisor goes exactly into 999.

(iii) From third division divisor multiplied by 9 or less produces 4 figures. ∴ divisor not 111. ∴ divisor is 333 or 999.

(iv) Consider third act of division (dividing into 1 – – 8). The biggest this could be is 1998. ∴ divisor not 999 ($2 \times 999 = 1998$ and there would be no remainder). ∴ divisor is 333. And first two divisions must obviously be 999.

(v) Consider last act of division. $333 \times x$ produces a number which, subtracted from y 000 leaves something between 1 and 9. Possible values of x are 6 ($333 \times 6 = 1998$), and 9($333 \times 9 = 2997$). If x were 6 last subtraction would be of 1998 from 2000. To produce 2 the previous multiple of 333 must end in 6 (bearing in mind that we are subtracting from 1 – – 8). The only possible multiple would be 333×2, but this only has 3 figures where there should be 4. ∴ x cannot be 6. ∴ x must be 9. And last subtraction must be of 2997 from 3000.

(vi) Figure to subtract from 8 to give 3 must be 5, and penultimate division is 333 × 5 (1665). Add up from bottom and complete solution is:

```
           300305·0̇0̇9
333)100001568
    999
    ---
     1015
      999
      ----
      1668
      1665
      ----
        3 000
        2 997
        -----
            3
        -----
```

31.

```
              – – –·– –
          ____________
  – – ) – – 5 – – .
          – –              (i)
        ______
          – – –            (ii)
          – – –            (v)
          ______
            – b 0
            – – –          (iv)
            ______
              a – 0        (iii)
              – – –
              ______
```

1. When there are no more figures to bring down a decimal point is put in answer and 0s are brought down, as shown.

2. Since (i) subtracted from – – 5 leaves only a single digit, – – 5 must be 105 and (i) must be between 96 and 99 inclusive.

3. (ii) must start with at least 6 (99 from 105) ∴ divisor greater than 6 – (since two figures are brought down). ∴ divisor 96, 97, 98 or 99.

4. From (iii) divisor goes exactly into – – 0, ∴ it must be 96 or 98. If 98, (iii) would be 490, and (iv) would end in 1. But no multiple of 98 ends in 1. ∴ divisor is 96. And since $5 \times 96 = 480$, ∴ $a = 4$, ∴ $b = 2$.

5. Since (iii) is 480, ∴ (iv) is – 72, and only possible multiple of divisor is 7×96 (672).

6. (ii) starts with $9(105 - 96)$. ∴ (v) must be 9×96 (864).

Rest follows easily:

```
        109·75
      ________
   96)10536
       96
       --
        936
        864
        ---
         72 0
         67 2
         ----
         4 80
         4 80
         ----
```

32.

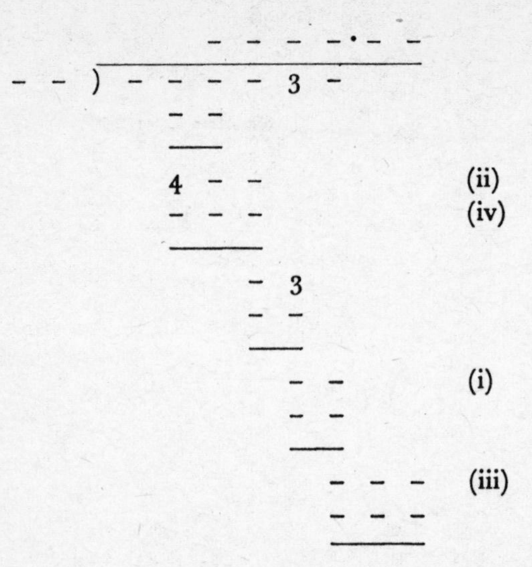

1. To go exactly into $x$oo (last division) divisor must end in 5 or 0. If it ends in 0, every multiple of it ends in 0, line (i) would have to be 3 –, and divisor must therefore be 30 or less. In this case a remainder of 4 – as in line (ii) would be impossible. ∴ divisor ends in 5.

2. To go exactly, less than 10 times, into $x$oo divisor must be 25 or 75. If 25 a remainder of 4 – as in line (ii) would be impossible. ∴ it is 75. ∴ two-figure multiples are 75

3. ∴ line (i) is result of subtracting 75 from – 3. This must be 83 and result of subtraction is 8.

4. Line (iii) must be 300 or 600 for 75 to go exactly less than 10 times. But 75 from 8 – cannot leave 3. ∴ Line (iii) must be 600.

5. Line (iv) must be a multiple of 75 starting in 4, ∴ 450.

Fill up from bottom and rest follows easily. Thus:

```
      1611·08
   ----------
75)120831
   75
   --
   458
   450
   ---
     83
     75
     --
      81
      75
      --
       6 00
       6 00
       ----
```

33.

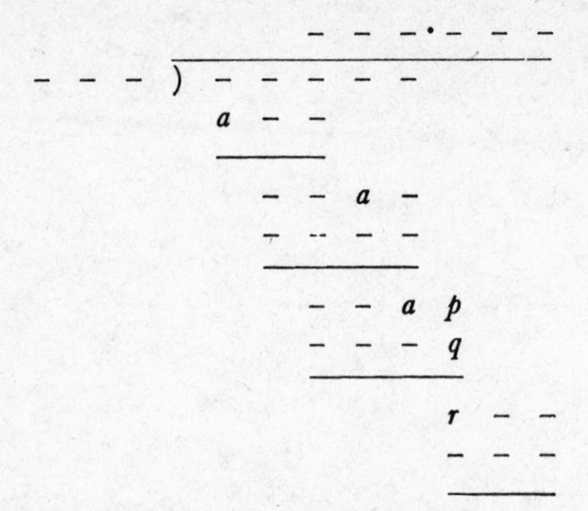

(i) p must be 0. ∴ q is not 0 (if it were, the last two rows would be 000, which would be absurd). ∴ divisor does not end in 0.

(ii) Since the divisor goes exactly, less than 10 times, into – 0 0, and does not end in 0, it must end in 5. ∴ q is 5, and r is 5.

(iii) It is easy to see that divisor must be 125.

(iv) $8 \times 125 = 1000$, ∴ 4-figure multiple ending in 5 can only be $9 \times 125 = 1125$.

(v) ∴ – – a p is $1125 + 5$ (i.e. 1130). ∴ $a = 3$.

(vi) ∴ first multiple of 125 must be 375 and rest follows easily.

Complete solution is:

```
       309·904
125)38738
     375
     ---
      1238
      1125
      ----
       1130
       1125
       ----
          500
          500
          ---
```

34.

```
                - - - - - - - -
        _______________________
- - - ) - - - - - -
        - - -                    (b)
        -----
            - - -
            - - -                (c)
            -----
              - - -
              - - -              (d)
              -----
                - - -
                - - a            (e)
                -----
                    - - - -
                    - - - -
                    -------

                    -------
```

(i) *a* cannot be 0. (The figure above it is 0, and if *a* were 0 the last two lines would be 0000, which would be absurd.)

(ii) ∴ divisor cannot end in 0. And since it goes exactly into – 000, it is easy to see that it must end in 5.

(iii) ∴ *a* must be 5; and last two rows must each be 5000.

(iv) ∴ divisor is a 3-figure number, ending in 5, which goes exactly, less than 10 times, into 5000. ∴ it is greater than 500. It is easy to see that it must be 625.

(v) If we multiply 625 by 2 or more we get more than 3 figures. ∴ rows *b*, *c*, *d*, and *e* must all be 625.

Fill these in, add up from the bottom and we get the complete solution:

```
      1011·1008
   ___________
625)631938
    625
    ---
     693
     625
     ---
      688
      625
      ---
       630
       625
       ---
         5000
         5000
         ----
```

35.

$$\text{(i)}\quad \begin{array}{r} d\ q\ c \\ p\ b \\ \hline s\ a \\ \hline \end{array} \qquad\qquad \text{(ii)}\quad \begin{array}{r} d\ q\ c \\ p\ b \\ \hline e\ r\ a \\ \hline \end{array}$$

Obviously (i) is subtraction and (ii) addition. Since $b - c = 1$, $\therefore$ from (i) $a = 9$.

Since b added to c and b subtracted from c produce the same digit, and there are no 0s, $\therefore$ $b = 5$, and $c = 4$.

From (i) $d = 1$ (if 2 or more, result of subtraction would be more than 100). In (ii), since e is not 1 (figures all different) $\therefore$ $e = 2$.

From (i) $p > q$; from (ii) $p + q > 12$. (There is not one to carry from $b + c$, and r cannot be 0, 1 or 2.)

If p is 6 or less, we cannot have $p > q$ and $p + q$ at least 12. $\therefore$ p can only be 7 or 8 ($a = 9$).

If $p = 8$, $q = 6$ or 7 (not 5 because $b = 5$).

If $p = 8$ and $q = 6$, then $r = 4$; but $c = 4$, and we are told that no two letters in (ii) are the same.

If $p = 8$ and $q = 7$, then $r = 5$; but $b = 5$. $\therefore$ p is not 8. $\therefore$ $p = 7$, $\therefore$ $q = 6$ ($p > q$ and $(p + q) > 12$). $\therefore$ $r = 3$, and $s = 8$.

Complete solution is:

$$\text{(i)}\quad \begin{array}{r} 164 \\ -75 \\ \hline 89 \\ \hline \end{array} \qquad\qquad \text{(ii)}\quad \begin{array}{r} 164 \\ +75 \\ \hline 239 \\ \hline \end{array}$$

36.

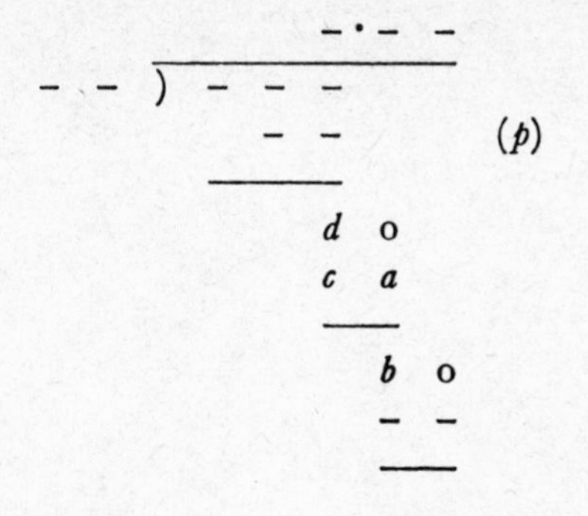

(i) Both figures brought down must be 0, as marked.

(ii) a cannot be 0. If it were, b would be 0, which would be absurd. ∴ divisor cannot end in 0.

(iii) If divisor ends in 5, then $a=5$ and $b=5$. ∴ divisor would be 25. But if divisor 25 it would go at least 4 times at first act of division, and (p) would contain three figures instead of two. ∴ divisor cannot end in 5.

(iv) For divisor to go exactly into b 0 it must end in 2, 4, 6 or 8 and it must go into b 0 five times. ∴ divisor must be 12, 14, 16 or 18.

(v) If divisor 14, $b=7$, and $a=3$, which is impossible.

(vi) If divisor 18, $b=9$, and $a=1$, which is impossible.

(vii) If divisor 12, $b=6$, and $a=4$. c a would then have to be 24 or 84. If c a were 24, d would be 3 and since p is 96, dividend would be 99. But dividend contains 3 figures, ∴ this is impossible.

(*Continued overleaf*)

If $c\ a$ were 84, d would be 9, and a solution is possible thus:

```
      8·75
   ------
12)105
    96
    --
    90
    84
    --
     60
     60
     --
```

(viii) If divisor 16, $b=8$, $a=2$, $c=3$, $d=4$.

And complete solution is:

```
      6·25
   ------
16)100
    96
    --
    40
    32
    --
     80
     80
     --
```

37.

$$\begin{array}{lrrrr} \text{(i)} & & c & d & e \\ & & & a & b \\ \hline & g & h & j & k \\ \hline \end{array} \qquad \begin{array}{lrrr} \text{(ii)} & c & d & e \\ & & a & b \\ \hline & b & l & a \\ \hline \end{array}$$

Digits are represented by letters.

(i) is obviously the addition and (ii) the subtraction.

The most that can be carried when two numbers are added is 1. $\therefore g=1$. Hence $c=9$ and $h=0$. From (ii), since c and b are different and $c=9$, $\therefore b=8$.

From (ii) $a>d$, and from (i) $a+d>10$ (there might be 1 to carry from $e+b$, but j cannot be 1). Bearing in mind that different letters stand for different digits a little trial and error will show that $a=7$, $d=4$. Since $b=8$, $\therefore b+e>10$, $\therefore j=2$ and $l=6$. It follows easily that $e=5$ and $k=3$.

Complete solution is therefore:

$$\begin{array}{lr} \text{(i)} & 945 \\ & 78 \\ \hline & 1023 \\ \hline \end{array} \qquad \begin{array}{lr} \text{(ii)} & 945 \\ & 78 \\ \hline & 867 \\ \hline \end{array}$$

38.

(i) Divisor goes exactly into $x00$ (see end) less than 10 times.

(ii) If divisor ended in 0, every multiple of it would end in 0, and d would have to be equal to a. We are told this is not so, ∴ divisor does not end in 0. ∴ divisor ends in 5 (otherwise a single figure multiple of it could not be $x00$.)

(iii) Easily seen that divisor must be 25 or 75 to go exactly into $x00$. If 25, the highest possible value of the first division would be 75. Subtracted from the 3-figure number this would leave 25 or more — which is absurd, ∴ divisor is not 25, ∴ divisor is 75.

(iv) ∴ each 2-figure multiple of divisor is 75.

(v) From a in quotient we see that $a = 1$.

(vi) Fill up other as, and from fact that each 2-figure multiple is 75, we see that $d = 6$.

(vii) 3 figures below a – – must be 150. (since $a = 1$.)

(viii) Since $b - c = 2$, and since $b\ c$ – must be multiple of 75 plus 7, it is easy to see that $b\ c$ – must be 532 (525 + 7.)

Fill in figures known, add up from the bottom, and solution is seen to be:

```
     1710211·08
75)128265831
   75
   —
   532
   525
   ——
     76
     75
     —
      158
      150
      ———
        83
        75
        —
         81
         75
         —
          6 00
          6 00
          ————

          ————
```

39.

1. Since the most that can be carried from adding 2 rows is 1, the 4-figure number must start 99 and the result of the addition must start 100.

2. Fill in 99 in the division:

```
          - - - - -
        ___________
  - - ) 9 9 - - 0 0
        - -           (i)
        ---
          a c -
            - -
          -----
              - 0 0
              - - -
              -----
                  -
              -----
```

3. *a* can only be 1 (a 2-figure number subtracted from *a c* – leaves less than 10). ∴ (i) must be 98. ∴ divisor must be 98 or a factor of 98.

4. *c* must be 0 (98 subtracted from 1 *c* – leaves less than 10.)

5. Addition now looks like this:

```
  9 9 0 -
      d -
  -------
1 0 0 - -
  -------
```

In order that there shall be 1 to carry from the column in which *d* is, *d* must be 9. ∴ divisor must be 98.

6. Division now looks like this:

```
         - - - - -
98 ) 9 9 0 e 0 0
     9 8
     ---
       1 0 -
         9 8
       -----
           - 0 0
           - - -
           -----
               -
           -----
```

and addition like this:

```
  9 9 0 e
      9 8
---------
1 0 0 0 -
---------
```

7. Consider addition: e must be at least 2, to produce 1 to carry.

8. Consider division: suppose e is 3. Then last act of division would be 98 into 500, which would go 5 times and leave a remainder of 10. But there is only 1 digit in remainder. $\therefore$ e cannot be 3 (even less can it be greater than 3). $\therefore$ $e = 2$, and rest follows easily.

```
    10104
98)990200
   98
   --
    102
     98
    ---
      400
      392
      ---
        8
      ---
```

```
 9902
   98
-----
10000
-----
```

40.

(i) Figure at the beginning of each line must be 1.

(ii) Multiplier must be 101 (only two rows of multiplication; middle one missing.)

Thus:

```
          - - - -
            1 0 1
          -------
          1 - - -
      1 a b c
  ---------------
  1 - - 1 - - -
  ---------------
```

(iii) a must be 1, for there must be 1 to carry from this column (in adding two rows together there can never be more than 1 to carry.)

(iv) Similarly b must be 1, for the sum of this column must be 11.

(v) c must also be 1, for there must be 1 to carry from this column, and there can be nothing to carry from column to right of c. $\therefore$ sum is 1111×101.

Thus:

```
   1111
    101
  -------
   1111
 1111
  -------
1001011
  -------
```

41.

```
               1 0 1 1
         ______________
1 - - 1 ) 1 - - - - - 1
          1 - - -
          -------
            1 - - -     (a)
            1 - - -     (b)
            -------
              1 - - -
              1 - - -
              -------

              -------
```

(i) Figure at the beginning of each number must be 1.

(ii) Quotient can be filled up as 1011 (0 is second digit because two figures have to be brought down.)

(iii) Because dividend ends in 1, divisor must also end in 1. (Figures so far have been filled in.)

(iv) If second figure in divisor were 1, the subtraction of *b* from *a* could not give 1 below second figures ∴ second figure in divisor is 0 and second figure in *a* must be 1.

(v) If third figure of divisor were 1, then subtraction of *b* from *a* would have to give 101 (in order that divisor should go exactly on the last division). But $1011 + 101 = 10000$, which cannot be right as *a* contains only 4 figures. ∴ third figure of divisor is not 1, and must be 0.

(*Continued overleaf*)

Rest follows easily.

```
          1011
     ________
1001)1100011
     1001
     ----
      1101
      1001
      ----
       1001
       1001
       ----

       ----
```

42.

(i) From *a* the sum must be less than 10 (decimal scale).

(ii) ∴ *c* must be to the scale of 2 (in no other scale can a number of four figures be less than ten). ∴ sum must be 8 or 9.

(iii) *b* must be to scale of 3 (not to scale of 2, since all scales are different; in no other scale can a number of 3 figures be less than ten). And sum in *b* must be 100 (i.e. 9). ∴ sum in *a* is 9, and in *c* is 1001.

(iv) first number in *c* must be 1 (the only single figure number.)

Second number in *b* at least 10 (i.e. 3) and since sum is 9, ∴ third number must be 5.

Final solution:

(*a*) *Scale of ten*	(*b*) *Scale of three*	(*c*) *Scale of two*
1	1	1
3	10	11
5	12	101
9	100	1001

43.

(All numbers on decimal scale, unless otherwise stated)

1. From (i) and (iii) number $\geqslant 10, < 36$.

2. If (ii) on scale of 3, number much greater than 36. ∴ (ii) on scale of 2, and number > 31. ∴ number must be 32, 33, 34 or 35.

3. (iv) obviously on binary scale. Larger factor at least 16. ∴ number not 33 (3×11), or 35 (5×7), or 32 (more than two prime factors). ∴ number must be 34 and rest follows easily.

Solution:

(i) 34 (on decimal scale) = (ii) 100010 (on the scale of 2) = (iii) 54 (on the scale of 6) = (iv) 10×10001 (on the scale of 2).

44. The Christmas Party

Number at least 22 (20 necessary for Strip the Pillow and at least 2 H's — since they are plural).

Number < 30 (see last sentence).

If 22, there must be 2 H's (since without them number must be a multiple of 5), and 2 J's (since with J's the number must be a multiple of 4 and there are less than 5 of each). But we are told that numbers of H's and J's are different.

If 23, there must be 3 H's, but only 1 J.

But there must be at least 2 J's, since they are plural.

If 24, 4 H's and 4 J's — but we are told numbers different.

If 25, we could play 'Strip the Pillow'. To play without H's there would have to be 5.

If 26. Only 1 H. But they are plural.

If 27, 2 H's; 1 or 5 J's (neither permissible).

If 28, we could play Bridge; first sentence absurd.

If 29, 4 H's and 3 J's. This is the only situation that fits the data.

∴ there were 29 people at the party.

(4 Higginbottles turned up, 3 Jones's failed to turn up.)

45. Alf, Bert and Charlie in the Classroom

A diagram for names and houses will be helpful.

		Houses				
		A	B	C	D	E
	A					
	B					
Names	C					
	D					
	E					

If B (i) true, B higher than E *and* C higher than E. ∴ E not higher than 3rd. ∴ E (i) false ('when making remarks about themselves only those who were 1st or 2nd tell the truth'). ∴ E higher than B, ∴ B (i) false.

But this is contrary to our assumption that B (i) true. ∴ B (i) false. ∴ E higher than C and E higher than B. ∴ E (i) false, ∴ E lower than 2nd.

Since B and C are both below E, ∴ E must be 3rd.

And A and D are both above E, B and C. ∴ A (i) true (since C is lower than A). ∴ B 4th and C 5th. ∴ E (ii) false, (since we know that A was higher than E). ∴ A not 1st, ∴ A 2nd and D 1st.

∴ order is: 1 = D, 2 = A, 3 = E, 4 = B, 5 = C.

∴ A (ii) false, ∴ D not in D house.

B (ii) false, ∴ D not in C house.

C (i) false, ∴ A not in C house.

C (ii) false, ∴ man in B house was 2nd, and was therefore A.

D (i) true, ∴ C in E house.

D (ii) true, ∴ E not in D house.

Since D is not in B, C, D or E houses, ∴ D is in A house. ∴ by elimination E is in C house, and B in D house.

∴ houses are: A in B house; B in D house; C in E house; D in A house; E in C house.

46. The Christmas Compensation Club

Use initial capitals for their ages. Facts given are:

$$(K - I) = 3(K - H) \qquad \text{(i)}$$

$$\frac{J}{H} = \frac{9}{10} \qquad \text{(ii)}$$

$$\frac{J}{I} = \frac{6}{5} \qquad \text{(iii)}$$

$$G - K = J - I \qquad \text{(iv)}$$

Since all letters must stand for whole numbers, ∴ from (ii) and (iii) J must be a multiple of 9 and of 6, ∴ a multiple of 18 (denote by m(18)). ∴ H is m(20), and I is m(15).

From (i) $2K = 3H - I$. (v)

∴ H and I must be both odd or both even (for 2K must be even).

But H is m(20) and cannot be odd. ∴ H and I both even, ∴ H is m(40) and I is m(30); ∴ J is m(36).

If H 80, I 60, and J 72, then from (v) $2K = 180$, ∴ $K = 90$.

But we are told that none of them has reached the age of 90. ∴ $H = 40$, $I = 30$, $J = 36$, $K = 45$, and from (iv) $G = 51$.

47. The Years Roll By

1. Consider B's remark. If true, it is false. (He cannot both be 81 and making a true statement). ∴ false. ∴ B under 50 or 64.

2. ∴ C's remark false. ∴ C under 50 or 64 or 81.

3. D (ii) true ∴ D over 50 or 27 and D (i) true. ∴ A is 57. ∴ A is truthful, ∴ E is 27. ∴ E is truthful, ∴ B older than A.

But B is under 50 or 64 (see (i)) and A is 57. ∴ B is 64.

4. E (ii) is true. D is 27 or over 50; C is 64, 81 or under 50, and D is 30 years younger than C. ∴ D is 51, and C is 81.

Ages are: A 57; B 64; C 81; D 51; E 27.

48. Sinister Street

(i) For A to claim that she knows where X lives she must certainly think his number is a perfect square. If she thinks it's a perfect square less than 50 there are too many alternatives (1, 4, 9, 16, etc.). But there are only *two* squares between 50 and 99 — namely 64 and 81. Clearly the only way in which A can claim to know X's number is if she lives in one of these houses and thinks X lives in the other. ∴ A's number is 64 or 81. X's number is *not* a square, greater than 50.

(ii) Since X answers B's second question truthfully, ∴ X must say his number is greater than 25. And for B to claim to know X's number she must certainly think it's a perfect cube. ∴ B must think X's number is 27 or 64, and she can only claim to know which if she lives in one of those houses herself. ∴ B's number is 27 or 64. X's number is not a cube.

(iii) Since X's number is greater than 50 and less than that of A or B. ∴ A's number must be 81, B's must be 64, and X's between 51 and 63 inclusive. The sum of their three numbers is a perfect square multiplied by 2. It is easy to see that this can only be 200. ∴ X's number is 55.

∴ A lives at No. 81; B lives at No. 64; X lives at No. 55.

49. Youthful Ambitions

Denote names of men by A_1, B_1, etc., wives by A_2, B_2, etc., birthplaces by A_3, B_3, etc., ambitions by A_4, B_4, etc.

A diagram will be helpful.

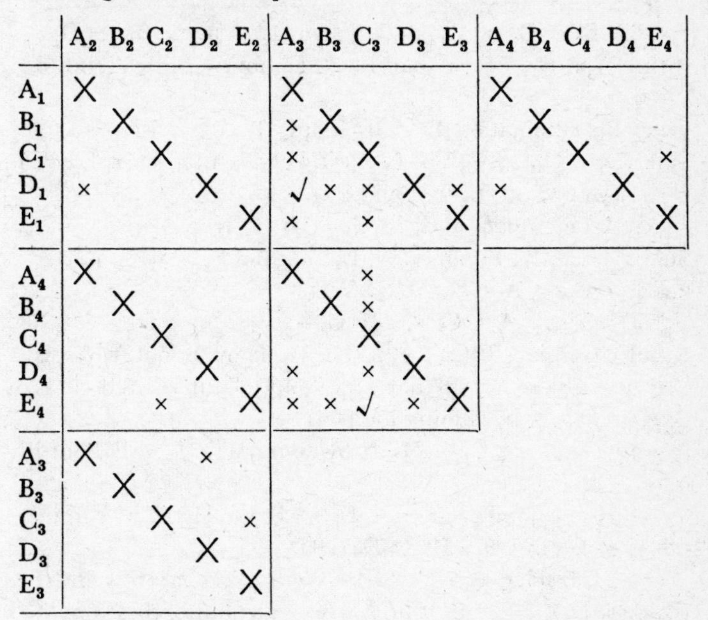

	A_2	B_2	C_2	D_2	E_2	A_3	B_3	C_3	D_3	E_3	A_4	B_4	C_4	D_4	E_4
A_1	X					X					X				
B_1		X				×	X					X			
C_1			X			×		X					X		×
D_1	×			X		✓	×	×	X	×	×			X	
E_1					X	×		×		X					X
A_4	X					X		×							
B_4		X					X	×							
C_4			X					X							
D_4				X		×		×	X						
E_4			×		X	×	×	✓	×	X					
A_3	X			×											
B_3		X													
C_3			X		×										
D_3				X											
E_3					X										

(i) Since for each man there are four different initial letters, ∴ we can cross out A_1, A_2; B_1, B_3, etc. as shown.

(ii) All E_2's remarks true (see conditions). ∴ from E_2 (2) C_3 is E_4 (mark in diagram, as shown). ∴ C_3 not A_4, B_4 etc. and E_4 not A_3, B_3, etc.

Since C_3 is E_4 and letters all different, ∴ C_3 not E_1 or E_2, and since E_4 is C_3 and letters all different, ∴ E_4 not C_1 or C_2.

(iii) E_2 (1) true. ∴ A_3 not B_1, and A_3 not E_1 (since remark is made by E_2).

(iv) Consider C_2's remark. The subject (A_3) not C_1.

(v) ∴ by elimination A_3 is D_1. ∴ A_3 not D_2 or D_4; D_1 not A_2 or A_4.

(Information so far has been marked in diagram. The reader may like to insert other information, as it is obtained, for himself.)

(vi) Since A_3 is D_1, ∴ C_2's remark false, ∴ A_3 not B_2.

(vii) A_2's remark false (see conditions), ∴ D_4 not B_2 and D_4 not A_1.

(viii) From B_2 (1) E_4 not B_1. From D_2's remark, B_4 not D_1.

(ix) A_3 is D_1; since A_3 not E_4, ∴ D_1 not E_4. Since A_3 not B_2, ∴ D_1 not B_2.

(x) By elimination D_1 is C_4. But D_1 is A_3, ∴ A_3 is C_4. Since D_1 is C_4, ∴ D_1 not C_2, ∴ by elimination D_1 is E_2. But D_1 is A_3 and C_4, ∴ E_2 is A_3 and C_4.

(xi) By elimination E_4 is A_1. ∴ B_2(1) true, ∴ E_4 not D_2. Since E_4 is A_1, ∴ E_4 not A_2, ∴ E_4 is B_2. But E_4 is A_1, ∴ B_2 is A_1, and E_4 is C_3, ∴ A_1 is C_3.

(xii) A_1 is B_2, A_1 is C_3 ∴ B_2 is C_3.

(xiii) Consider B_2(2). (B_3 is D_4). We know B_3 not A_1 (C_3 is), ∴ remark false. ∴ B_3 not D_4, ∴ by elimination B_3 is A_4. ∴ A_4 not B_1, ∴ by elimination D_4 is B_1.

(xiv) ∴ B_1 not D_2 or D_3 ∴ by elimination B_1 is E_3. But B_1 is D_4, ∴ E_3 is D_4.

(xv) ∴ by elimination B_4 is D_3. ∴ B_4 not D_2, ∴ by elimination A_4 is D_2. But A_4 is B_3, ∴ D_2 is B_3.

(xvi) Consider D_2's remark. We know that this is true (B_4 is *not* D_2). ∴ B_4 must be A_1, B_1 or C_1; but of these only C_1 is possible. ∴ B_4 is C_1. ∴ B_4 not C_2. ∴ by elimination B_4 is A_2 and ∴ C_1 is A_2.

(xvii) ∴ by elimination D_2 is E_1, and C_2 is B_1. D_4 is C_2. B_1 is E_3 ∴ C_2 is E_3. ∴ by elimination A_2 is D_3, and ∴ C_1 is D_3. ∴ E_1 is B_3 and E_1 is A_4.

Complete solution:

Arthur	Barbara	Chippenham	Entomologist
Basil	Clarissa	Ealing	Dog-fancier
Clarence	Alice	Delhi	Barber
Dudley	Eve	Andover	Cheese-parer
Ethelred	Dorothy	Bristol	Anarchist

50. Alpha Avenue

('m (3)' denotes 'multiple of 3'; '$\overline{\text{m}}$ (3)' denotes '*not* a multiple of 3'; $\overline{\text{sq}}$ denotes '*not* a perfect square' . . . etc).

After hearing the answers of A, B and C, Q must think that the number is in one of the following categories:

(i)	sq;	m (3);	1 fig.	*Possibilities*	9
(ii)	sq;	m (3);	2 figs.	,,	36, 81
(iii)	sq;	$\overline{\text{m}}$ (3);	1 fig.	,,	4
(iv)	sq;	$\overline{\text{m}}$ (3);	2 figs.	,,	16, 25, 49, 64
(v)	$\overline{\text{sq}}$;	m (3);	1 fig.	,,	3, 6
(vi)	$\overline{\text{sq}}$;	$\overline{\text{m}}$ (3);	1 fig.	,,	5, 7, 8
(vii)	$\overline{\text{sq}}$;	m (3);	2 figs.	,,	12, 15, 18 . . . etc.
(viii)	$\overline{\text{sq}}$;	$\overline{\text{m}}$ (3);	2 figs.	,,	11, 13, 14 . . . etc.

Q thinks that *he might be certain* about the number if he knew whether it was *m* (5).

The only two possible categories for the number to be in for him to say this are (iv) and (vi). In both cases he would know what the number was if he were told that it was m (5), but would still be uncertain if he were told that it was $\overline{\text{m}}$ (5).

Since in fact (from his next remark) he is still uncertain, he must have been told $\overline{\text{m}}$ (5). He now says 'If I knew whether the number was odd or even . . .', and he must therefore think that number is in category (vi) and *not* (iv).

(If he thought that it was in category (iv) and was told that it was even, he would not know whether it was 16 or 64).

We do not know whether he was told that it was odd or even, and therefore whether the house at which he called was number 7 or 8.

But in fact, as Alf and Bert both lied, we know that the correct number must be sq; m (3); 1 fig. ∴ *it can only be 9.*

51. Vestites Revealed

The essential point here is that B *is able* to make certain deductions. We must therefore consider his state of mind, what he must know.

If B knows that A and he both have the same politics, he can deduce that C's are different ('at least one of each'). But if he knows that A's politics are different from his own he cannot deduce C's. Similarly with nationalities.

It must be in this way that B deduces C's politics and religion.

B is not told whether A is Vestite or Transvestite, and therefore he cannot discover which C is by this method. But if B knows that C is any two of Irish, Liberal, Transvestite he can deduce that he can't be the third. And this is the *only way* in which B can deduce whether C is Vestite or Transvestite.

Therefore B must know that C is Irish and Liberal, and deduce that he is Vestite.

B can only know that C is Irish if A and he are both English.

B can only know that C is Liberal if A and he are both Conservative.

B is also able to deduce whether A is Vestite or Transvestite. He can only do this if he (B) is the same as C, whom he knows to be Vestite.

Therefore B must also be Vestite and he deduces that A must be Transvestite.

Complete solution:

A	B	C
English	English	Irish
Conservative	Conservative	Liberal
Transvestite	Vestite	Vestite

52. Uncle Knows Best

We are clearly only interested in those answers to (i), (ii) and (iii) which reduce the possible alternatives to a small number.

These are:

	(i)	(ii)	(iii)	Numbers
(*a*)	Yes	Yes	Yes	36
(*b*)	Yes	Yes	No	16, 64, 100
(*c*)	Yes	No	Yes	72
(*d*)	No	Yes	Yes	9, 81
(*e*)	No	Yes	No	25, 49

1. Consider B's remark to X. B must think that X's number is one of two, one of which is greater than 83, but not the other. The only category in which this is possible is *b*. But here there are two alternatives less than 81. The only possibility is for B to be one of them. ∴ B's number must be 16 or 64; and he must think that X is the other of these or 100. C hears, and knowing B's number as well as his own is able to write down X's number correctly. This is only possible if C himself lives in 16, 64, or 100.

2. Consider B's remark to Y. B must think that Y's number is one of two, one of which is greater than 50 but not the other. Remembering that no two sets of answers are exactly the same, this can only be in category *d*. ∴ Y's number is 9 or 81. C knows that Y's number is greater than his (and we know that C's number is 16, 64 or 100). ∴ Y's number must be 81 and C's number must be 16 or 64.

3. Consider B's remark to Z. Number must be one of two, one of which is greater than 30 but not the other. Since no two sets of answers are exactly the same, this can only be in category *e*. ∴ Z's number is 25 or 49. C notes that his number is less than Z's, ∴ his (C's) must be 16 and not 64; B's number is 64, and X's number is 100. And C guesses, correctly, that Z's number is greater than 30. ∴ Z's number is 49.

Complete solution: Bartholomew = 64; Claudius = 16; X = 100; Y = 81; Z = 49.

53. Acacia Avenue

The method must obviously be to make inferences from what A, B and C say, about where they themselves live. Thus:

1. The only information A has about B's number is whether it is a multiple of 23 and that it is higher than his own. It is only possible for A to claim to know with certainty where B lives if A himself lives between 23 and 45 inclusive, and thinks (not necessarily correctly) that B's number is 46.

2. B's information about A's number is whether it is a perfect cube and that it is less than his own. It is only possible for B to claim to know with certainty where A lives if B himself lives between 9 and 27 inclusive and thinks (not necessarily correctly) that A's number is 8.

3. Since A's number is not less than 23, and B's number is not greater than 27 and the difference between their numbers is at least 4. ∴ A must live at 23, and B at 27.

4. Similarly since A claims to know that C must live in one of two houses, and since he thinks that B's number is 46, he must obviously think that C's number is a perfect square, greater than B's, and he must therefore think that C's number is 49 or 64.

We are told that A is right in what he thinks about C's number being a perfect square. ∴ C's number is a perfect square, and it is greater than 27.

5. A claims that C's number is 49 or 64. But we are told that all the answers written down are wrong.

∴ C's number must be 36. (the only other perfect square between 27 and 65.)

∴	A	23
	B	27
	C	36

54. The Willahs and the Wallahs

(i) C to E: 'I'm a Willah.' If true, this is spoken by a Willah to a Willah. If false, it is spoken by a Wallah to a Willah. In both cases E must be a Willah.

(ii) E to B: 'My number is 35.' Since E is a Willah whose numbers are prime this is false. ∴ B is a Wallah.

(iii) E to A: 'I'm a Wallah.' This is false. ∴ A is a Wallah.

(iv) A to B: 'D is a Wallah.' Since A and B are both Wallahs this is true. And since there are 3 of each tribe, A, B, D are Wallahs; C, E, F are Willahs.

(v) F to C. true. ∴ $F - C = 10$.

(vi) B to D true. ∴ F's number halfway between D's and C's. ∴ $D - F = 10$.

(vii) C to F true. ∴ D's number halfway between A's and F's. ∴ $A - D = 10$, and $D - F = 10$, and $F - C = 10$.

And the numbers of A, D, F and C must all be less than 50 (see D to A). A's and D's are *not* primes; F's and C's are primes. ∴ the numbers of A, D, F, C are such that each is greater by 10 than the following one, all are less than 50. A's and D's are not prime numbers; F's and C's are. A little investigation shows that the only possibilities are 49, 39, 29, 19 in that order.

Complete solution is therefore: A, Wallah (not prime) = 49; B, Wallah (not prime) = ?; C, Willah (prime) = 19; D, Wallah (not prime) = 39; E, Willah (prime) = ?; F, Willah (prime) = 29.

The exact numbers of B and E cannot be discovered.

55. Out of the Window and Over the Wall

Set out the times at which the sentries starting from P_1, Q_1, R_1, S_1 are out of range (i.e. more than 100 yards away).

P_1	Q_1	R_1	S_1
9.0 —9.4	9.0½ —9.9½	9.0 —9.2	9.1 —9.7
9.7 —9.15	9.10½—9.19½	9.4 —9.8	9.9 —9.15
9.18—9.26	9.20½—9.29½	9.10—9.14	9.17—9.23
9.29—9.37	9.30½—9.39½	9.16—9.20	9.25—9.31
9.40—9.48	9.40½—9.49½	9.22—9.26	9.33—9.39
		9.28—9.32	9.41—9.47
		9.34—9.38	
		9.40—9.44	

We have to find the first three periods of 2 minutes or more which are common to all these.

They are: (i) 9.10½ (till 9.14); (ii) 9.34 (till 9.37); (iii) 9.41 (till 9.44).

56. The World of Bonkers

1. Put information about numbers of days in months in a more convenient form:

Cucumber	19
Strawberry	19
Tiddleywinks	17
Jinks	17
Pinafore	10
Collywobble	13 (even years) 44 (odd years)
Stephen	4 (if year's date does not end in 7) 6 (if year's date ends in 7)

Consider first piece of information.

From Funday, Strawberry 17th to Blissday, Tiddleywinks 8th is just over 7 weeks, ∴ Funday, Strawberry 17th to Funday, Tiddleywinks 6th is exactly 7 weeks (35 days). Of these days 8(2 + 6) are in Strawberry and Tiddleywinks, leaving 27 for other months. The only possibility in this year is Jinks (17) and Pinafore (10).

∴ we have (i) Strawberry
(Jinks
Pinafore)
Tiddleywinks

These are consecutive months, but we don't yet know whether Jinks or Pinafore comes first.

Consider other information. There are 50 days from Collywobble 41st to Pinafore 7th. 10 of these days (3 + 7) are in Collywobble and Pinafore, leaving 40 for intervening months. Stephen only has 4 days this year, and the only combination of months that can produce 40 is Strawberry or Cucumber (19), Jinks or Tiddleywinks (17), and Stephen (4).

∴we have: (ii) Collywobble
(Strawberry or Cucumber
Jinks or Tiddleywinks
Stephen)
Pinafore

We do not yet know the order of the intervening months.

From (i) we know that Jinks comes before Tiddleywinks and from (ii) we know that Jinks comes before Pinafore. From (ii) we see that Collywobble and Stephen must, in that order, come before the four mentioned in (i). Since we know that Collywobble is the first month of the year, the remaining month, Cucumber, must be last.

Order is: Collywobble
Stephen
Strawberry
Jinks
Pinafore
Tiddleywinks
Cucumber

2. Collywobble 2nd comes before Strawberry 13th. Since it is the year 21 there are 44 days in Collywobble and 4 in Stephen. ∴ number of days is $42 + 4 + 13 = 59$ — i.e. 11 weeks and 4 days. 4 days before Workday is Joyday.

57.

(i) 8 across can only be 27. ∴ last two digits of 4 down must be 89.

(ii) ∴ first digit of 11 across is 9. And since 11 across is same when reversed, and sum of digits is divisible by 9 (because number is divisible by 9), ∴ it can only be 9999.

(iii) 3 down must be 512 (the only 3-figure cube ending in 2).

(iv) ∴ sum of digits of 5 across is 4 (half cube root of 512). ∴ other two digits must be 1 and 2 (no 0s). And since 2 down must be odd (a prime number), ∴ 5 across is 112. ∴ first digit of 4 down is 1.

(v) Sum of digits of 10 down can only be 16, ∴ 10 down is 79.

(vi) For 9 across we want a 3-figure square of an even number, starting with 7. This can only be 28^2 (784), ∴ 9 across is 487.

(vii) 7 down can only be 189 (27×7).

(viii) First digit of 1 across can only be 7 (see also 1 down). ∴ 2 down must be 31, and 1 across is 79351.

(ix) See 1 down and 6 across must be 11, and 1 down 721.

Complete solution:

(1) 7	9	(2) 3	(3) 5	(4) 1
2	■	(5) 1	1	2
(6) 1	(7) 1	■	(8) 2	7
(9) 4	8	(10) 7	■	8
■	(11) 9	9	9	9

58.

(i) Starting point provided by 7 across in conjunction with 4 down. First digit of 7 across cannot be less than 3 (see 4 down and remember that there are no 0s). $\therefore$ 7 across is 34; and first three digits of 4 down are 1 2 3.

(ii) Consider 8 down in conjunction with 11 across. 8 down must be 441.

(iii) Consider 10 across. One of the primes must be 2 (number is even). A little trial shows that it can only be $(2 \times 11)^2 = 484$.

(iv) $\therefore$ last digit of 4 down is 9 (>8).

(v) Consider 10 down and 1 across. 10 down can only be 41, 43 or 47. For square to end in 1, it must be 41. And 1 across must be $(41)^2 = 1681$.

(vi) 1 down can only be 125.

(vii) 3 down can only be 83 or 89. From 5 across we see that it must be 83. And 5 across is 2532.

Rest follows easily:

[1] 1	[2] 6	[3] 8	[4] 1	■
[5] 2	5	3	2	■
[6] 5	1	■	[7] 3	[8] 4
[9] 2	7	[10] 4	8	4
3	■	[11] 1	9	1

59.

(i) 4 down can only be the cube of 8 (512). (The cube of 27 contains more than 3 figures).

(ii) Consider 1 across, 4 across and 9 across. 1 across is a cube (4 across) and a multiple of 9 across, which is a multiple of 9 (sum of digits = 9). And since 1 across is *odd*, it can only be the cube of 9 (729). 9 across is not a cube and is a factor of 729. It can only be 81. 4 across is 54 (6×9).

(iii) From 1 down, 5 across starts with 8 and 11 across with 7.

(iv) 5 across must start at least 81 (there are no 0s). ∴ its square root is 9 –. And since it ends in 1, and is the product of *two* primes it must be the square of 91. (8281).

(v) 11 across must be 71, 73 or 79. But from 2 down 71 and 73 not possible. ∴ 11 across is 79, and 2 down is 22619.

(vi) Consider 6 across. 3-figure squares with 6 as second figure are 169, 361, 961. But 169 is not possible (see 3 down), and 961 is greater than 1 across. ∴ 6 across is 361.

(vii) 7 across can be 21, 24 or 27. If 21, 8 down is 158, which makes 12 across even. If 24, 8 down is 474, which makes 12 across even. ∴ 7 across is 27, which makes 8 down 711.

(viii) From 10 down, second digit of 12 across must be 1. 10 across can be 31, 41, 61, 71. But if 10 across 31, 12 across is 211, and ∴ not odd when reversed. Similarly 10 across cannot be 71. ∴ 12 across is 311 or 511, but 511 (7×73) is not prime. ∴ 12 across is 311, and 10 across is 41.

Complete solution:

(1) 7	(2) 2	(3) 9	(4) 5	4
(5) 8	2	8	1	■
(6) 3	6	1	(7) 2	(8) 7
(9) 8	1	■	(10) 4	1
(11) 7	9	(12) 3	1	1

60.

(i) Consider 7 across. The only digits that are meaningful in a mirror are 0, 1, 8. We are told there are no 0s, and that when we look at 7 across in a mirror what we see is smaller. ∴ 7 across must be 81 (18 in a mirror).

(ii) 8 down must be 127 (125 is only 3-figure cube starting with 1).

(iii) 12 across. Age 8 years ago is a perfect square ending in 9. This could be 9 or 49. 9 obviously absurd, ∴ 49, ∴ 12 across is 57.

(iv) 10 down must be a multiple of 3. ∴ 15, 45 or 75. 9 across makes 15 or 75 impossible, ∴ 45. ∴ 9 across is 642.

(v) 4 down. Since cube ends in 8 it must be cube of a number ending in 2. And cube must be between 1000 and 2000. This can only be 12^3 (1728). ∴ 4 down is 728.

(vi) 5 across is a 4-figure multiple of 321 ending in 2. ∴ we must multiply by 12, 22, 32, etc. But 321 × 32 contains 5 figures, and 321 × 22 contains a 0. ∴ 321 × 12 (3852).

(vii) 9 down must be 69 (6 turned upside down becomes 9).

(viii) 2 down. An odd square (see 6 across) with 8 as second digit. This can only be 289.

(ix) 3 down. This must be a multiple of 19. ∴ 95.

(x) 1 across. This must end in 5, since it is a multiple of 5 and there are no 0s. Sum of digits divisible by 9 (since a multiple of 9). ∴ 1st digit is 4 and number is 42975.

(xi) 11 across could be 469 or 139. But 5 down must end in odd digit. ∴ 11 across is 139 ∴ 2nd digit of 5 down is 5, and 5 down is 3571.

Complete solution:

4	2	9	7	5
3	8	5	2	■
5	9	■	8	1
7	■	6	4	2
1	3	9	5	7

61.

(i) The only clue which has a unique solution before we find answers to other clues is 12 down. This can only be 72.

(ii) The only 3-figure cube ending in 2 is the cube of 8. ∴ 14 across is 512.

(iii) 11 across is 67 ($4 \times 19 = 76$).

(iv) Since 8 down ends in 1, the factor of 76 must be odd (19), ∴ 8 down is 361 (see also 9 down).

Rest follows easily.

62.

(i) 7 across provides a starting point. 36 and 81 are the only 2-figure squares which are multiples of sum of digits. 81 not possible because of 5 down. ∴ 7 across is 36.

(ii) ∴ last 3 digits of 5 down are 7, 8, 9.

(iii) 8 across must be 27. ∴ 4 down must be 432.

(iv) 13 across must be 49.

(v) 3 across is a multiple of 49, ending with a digit less than 6 (see 5 down), and having 4 as its second digit. Possibilities are 245 (5×49), 343 (7×49) and 441 (9×49). But 1st digit of 3 across is same as last digit of 6 across (see 3 down) and 6 across is a perfect square. But no square ends in 2 or 3. ∴ 3 across is 441.

Rest follows easily.

1: 1	2: 1	3: 4	4: 4	5: 1
6: 4	8	4	7: 3	6
4	6	■	8: 2	7
■	9: 9	10: 9	11: 5	8
12: 6	3	8	13: 4	9

63.

(i) 10 down could be 12, 24, 36, 48. 13 across is a perfect cube and could therefore start with 1, 2, 3, 5, 7. The only one of these which can be the second figure of 10 down is 2. ∴ 10 down is 12, and 13 across is 216.

(ii) ∴ 8 across starts with 1.

(iii) Consider 7 down and 8 across. $\frac{1}{3}$ of 8 across (1 – 1) must end in 7, and must be 37, 47 or 57. ∴ 7 down is a multiple of 37, 47 or 57 ending in 6, and starting with an odd digit (since 6 across is a prime number). A little investigation will show that it can only be 8 × 47 (376), and 8 across must be 3 × 47 = 141.

(iv) ∴ first digit of 11 across is 6.

(v) ∴ first three digits of 4 down must be 9, 8, 7.

(vi) 5 across. The only 4-figure perfect cube ending in 8 is cube of 12 (1728).

(vii) 2 down must start with even digit (twice a prime number when reversed). 72, 76, 78 are not twice a prime number; 74 is. ∴ 2 down is 47.

(viii) 9 down must be 42 or 48. If 42, 12 across would have to be 32 or 92 (a prime number when reversed), but neither of these is twice a prime number, ∴ 9 down is 48, and 12 across can only be 38.

(ix) 1 down. Least prime number greater than 19 is 23. The two missing digits in 1 down would then be 9 and 9. And this is the only possibility.

(x) Since 1 across is odd it must end in 9.

(xi) 3 down must be 42– or 92– (see 1 across). 92– cannot be a multiple of 61, but 427 is.

9	4	4	9	9
1	7	2	8	
9		7	7	3
1	4	1	6	7
3	8	2	1	6

64. The Double Cross-Number

(i) Consider 6 down (a cube) and 9 across (a square). There are only two 3-figure cubes such that the second digit is the first digit of the square of the cube root. These are 125 (square of cube root is 25) and 343 (square of cube root is 49). Let us put 125 and 25 in A, and 343 and 49 in B.

(ii) 10 down in B can only be 97; in A it can be 53 or 59. (Put both 3 and 9 down as alternatives.)

(iii) 6 across in B must be $4 \times 97 = 388$. In A, 6 across cannot be 2×53 (106) because there are no 0s. ∴ 10 down must be 59, and 6 across is $2 \times 59 = 118$.

(iv) Consider 2 down (B). The only 3-figure square starting with 8 is 841. ∴ 2 down is 148. 2 down (A) can either be 121 (11^2) reversed or 169 (13^2) reversed. Mark in both alternatives.

(v) 5 across. In B this can only be 484. In A this cannot start with 2 (no perfect square ends in 2), ∴ it starts with 6 and can only be 676. And 2 down must be 961.

(vi) 1 across can only be 39 in A and 11 in B.

(vii) 4 down. (A) 3-figure squares with 2nd figure 6 are 169, 361, 961. (B) 3-figure squares with 2nd figure 4 are 144, 441, 841. In A answer could be 169 or 961. In B it must be 841. But 7 across in A has to be a multiple of 48 ∴ it cannot start with 1. ∴ 4 down must be 169.

(viii) 7 across must be 96 in A and 14 in B.

(ix) 8 down (A). Last digit cannot be 9 (digits of 13 across all different and we already have a 9). ∴ it must be 691. In B 8 down must obviously be 481 (see 13 across).

(x) 11 across must start with 9 in A, and 8 in B.

(xi) Consider 3 down in B. Other two digits add up to at least 16. Last digit (see 13 across) is either 5 or 9. ∴ not 5 but 9. 13 across must be 37951, and 1st digit of 3 down can be 7, 8 or 9.

(xii) Consider 3 down in A. Other two digits add up to at least 16. Last digit (see 13 across) is either 3 or 7. ∴ not 3 but 7. ∴ 13 across is 59731, and 1st digit of 3 down must be 9.

(xiii) Consider 3 across. In A it must be 919. In B 1st and last digits add up to 8, 1st is 7, 8 or 9 and there are no 0s. ∴ 3 across must be 781.

(xiv) 12 down in A. 32 a factor of 96. ∴ 12 down is 23. 12 down in B. 56 a multiple of 14. ∴ 12 down is 65.

A

[1] 3	[2] 9	[3] 9	[4] 1	9
■	[5] 6	7	6	■
[6] 1	1	8	[7] 9	[8] 6
[9] 2	[10] 5	[11] 9	[12] 2	9
[13] 5	9	7	3	1

B

[1] 1	[2] 1	[3] 7	[4] 8	1
■	[5] 4	8	4	■
[6] 3	8	8	[7] 1	[8] 4
[9] 4	[10] 9	[11] 8	[12] 6	8
[13] 3	7	9	5	1

65. Mathematics, English and French

(i) First. If A beats everyone at each subject separately, he must also beat everyone at all subjects combined.

(ii) The place for English could have been anything from 1st to 23rd. The marks lost by being low in English (E) can be more than made up by the higher marks in Mathematics (M) and French (F).

(iii) Let person whose places were 2nd, 5th, 6th be B. 1 person beat B at M, 4 at E and 5 at F.

Even if these people were all different not more than 10 people beat B at anything. ∴ combined place is not lower than 11th. B could easily have beaten *everybody* at something (he beat 21 at M, 18 at E, 17 at F), ∴ he could have beaten everybody in the combined order. ∴ combined place could be anything between 1st and 11th inclusive.

(iv) Argument similar to (iii). Let person be C. C beat 6 at M, 2 at E, 0 at F. ∴ not more than 8 altogether. ∴ combined place is not higher than 15th. Obviously no lower limit. ∴ combined place between 15th and 23rd inclusive.

(v) Let person be D. In order to be 1st in combined order D must have beaten other 22 at *one* subject at least. D beat 6 at M and 4 at E; ∴ D must have beaten at least 12 at F. ∴ place for F is not lower than 11th. ∴ place must be between 1st and 11th (inclusive).

66. The Deception Test

(i) Consider C's remark. If false he was last, but if false he was 1st or 2nd. ∴ remark true, ∴ C not 1st or 2nd and not last.

(ii) If E true, then B false; ∴ E 1st, ∴ E not true, ∴ E false. ∴ E 1st or 2nd and since E false, ∴ B not 2nd.

(iii) If B false, E 1st and B 1st or 2nd (because remark false). But B not 2nd, ∴ E and B both 1st, which is impossible. ∴ B true. ∴ E 2nd and B not 1st.

(iv) ∴ either A or D 1st (no one else can be). If A true, D not 1st, ∴ A 1st, ∴ A false. ∴ A not true. ∴ D not 3rd and A 1st (since he lies.)

(v) D not 1st or 2nd, ∴ D truthful. ∴ C lower than B. C can only be 3rd or 4th (see (i)) and B not 1st or 2nd. ∴ B 3rd and C 4th. ∴ D 5th.

∴ Order is: 1 A; 2 E; 3 B; 4 C; 5 D.

67. Who Beat Whom?

If C thought that B was lying and A truthful, he could not possibly have deduced the places correctly.

∴ he must think B truthful and A lying (and we know that he is right.)

∴ he knows A is 2nd, B 2 places higher than D, and his own place.

If C 3rd, there is no way in which B can be 2 places higher than D. ∴ C not 3rd. If C 4th he would not know whether B 1st and D 3rd or B 3rd and C 5th. But he does know, ∴ C not 4th.

We are told C not 5th. ∴ C 1st, A 2nd, B and D must be 3rd and 5th and ∴ E 4th.

Thus: 1 C; 2 A; 3 B; 4 E; 5 D.

68. The Race is to the Ruthless

(i) For C(1) to be true, E, B or C must have been 3rd, ∴ C(2) false. ∴ as C(1) and C(2) cannot both be true, C is a liar, his remarks are both false, and D's remarks are both true.

(ii) ∴ C is one place higher than D.

(iii) ∴ C not 5th, and from D(1) A not 5th. ∴ from D(2) B must be 1st or 2nd (A and C can't be lower than 3rd and 4th).

(iv) Suppose B 2nd, then A 3rd, C 4th and D 5th (see (ii)). ∴ E 1st. But A is not now half-way between C and E (D(1)) ∴ B not 2nd. ∴ B 1st.

(v) ∴ order must be: 1 B; 2 E; 3 A; 4 C; 5 D.

69. The Brainstorm Brothers

We must think about the state of Casanova's mind.

He knows: (i) that Charles was 2 places higher than Clarence; (ii) that Terence was not 1st; (iii) his own place.

With this information he can determine everyone's place.

Charles and Clarence could have been 1st and 3rd, 2nd and 4th, 3rd and 5th. If Casanova was 3rd they could *only* have been 2nd and 4th, if he was anywhere else he could not know their places. ∴ Casanova must have been 3rd, Charles 2nd and Clarence 4th. Terence was not 1st, ∴ he was 5th. And Claud was 1st.

Thus: 1 Claud; 2 Charles; 3 Casanova; 4 Clarence; 5 Terence.

70. The Efficiency Test

(i) B's remark cannot be true — if true he would have to be 1st. ∴ B not 1st or 3rd.

(ii) C's remark cannot be true — if true C would have to be 1st, not D. ∴ neither C nor D 1st.

(iii) ∴ D's remark false, ∴ B not 2nd.

(iv) ∴ B not 1st, 2nd or 3rd; ∴ A's remark cannot be true, ∴ A not 1st.

(v) ∴ E must be 1st (no one else is). ∴ E's remark true, ∴ A 2nd and C 5th, ∴ B 4th (see (iv)), ∴ D 3rd.

∴ order is: 1 E; 2 A; 3 D; 4 B; 5 C.

71. Bert goes Psychic

C thinks *either* (i) that A was *not* 2nd and that B was *not* 2 places higher than D,

or (ii) that A *was* 2nd and that B *was* 2 places higher than D.

From (i) *or* (ii) and his own place he claims to be able to announce order of merit for all five.

He clearly could not do this from (i) and his own place; therefore it must be from (ii) and his own place.

∴ possible places of B and D are 1st and 3rd or 3rd and 5th. To be able to eliminate one of these alternatives C must have been 1st or 5th. But we know that C must be 4th or 5th (he could not get his own place wrong). ∴ C was 5th. ∴ order C announced must have been: B, A, D, E, C.

But this is wrong — only last two are in the correct places. ∴ order of first three is *either* A, D, B *or* D, B, A (in no other order would all three have been predicted incorrectly). But A and B are placed in the order of their truthfulness. A was certainly truthful (not 2nd) and B certainly untruthful (not two places higher than D). ∴ A higher than B.

∴ correct order is: A, D, B, E, C.

72. The Ladies' Tests

We must first consider what we can say about Q's places from the fact that with P's information (higher for F than for C or I) she was able to deduce order of merit for each subject.

In fact there are several possibilities for this.

If Q was 2nd for F, then P must have been 1st for F (in order to be higher for F than for C or I). And P could have been 2nd or 3rd for C and I. Q will know which if *she* is 2nd or 3rd for C and I, but not otherwise. ∴ P and Q must between them be 2nd and 3rd for C and I, and ∴ R must be 1st for both.

But we are told that R is higher for C than for I.

∴ Q was not 2nd for F.

If Q were 3rd for F she would have no way of knowing whether P was 1st or 2nd.

∴ Q must have been 1st for F.

∴ P must have been 2nd for F.

And R must have been 3rd for F.

And P must have been 3rd for both C and I. Q must therefore have been 1st or 2nd for C and I, and whichever she is she will know that R is the other.

Since we are told that R is higher for C than for I, ∴ R must have been 1st for C and 2nd for I, and Q must have been 1st for I and 2nd for C.

∴ orders are:

	Charm		*Femininity*		*Intuition*
1.	R	1.	Q	1.	Q
2.	Q	2.	P	2.	R
3.	P	3.	R	3.	P

73. Latin, Greek and Mathematics

A diagram will help.

	L	G	M
1			C
2	C		
3		C	
4	E		
5			E

From (iii) C is 3rd, 4th or 5th at G.

From (iv) C is 1st, 2nd, or 3rd at G. ∴ C must be 3rd at G.

From (iii) C is 1st at M and 2nd at L (mark these facts in diagram as shown).

From (iv) E is 4th at L and 5th at M (these facts too have been marked in).

The reader may like to insert other facts as they are discovered.

From (i) D not 2nd at G (because A not 1st at L) and D not 5th. ∴ D must be 4th at G; and A 3rd at L.

Consider (v). Sum of C's places $=6$ $(1+2+3)$. ∴ sum of D's $=9$.

D 4th at G, ∴ sum of other two places $=5$ $(1+4$ or $2+3)$. $(2+3)$ not possible (2, 3, and 4 in L already filled). ∴ D 1st at L and 4th at M. ∴ B 5th at L (other places filled).

From (ii) B's other two places add up to 4, and they can only be 2nd and 2nd. ∴ A 3rd at M (other places filled).

And since order is in no case completely alphabetical, E must be 1st and A 5th at G.

∴ orders are:

	Latin	*Greek*	*Mathematics*
1.	D	E	C
2.	C	B	B
3.	A	C	A
4.	E	D	D
5.	B	A	E

74. Honesty, Intelligence and Charm

1. Consider C(i). If true, then false, (the man who is 4th for Honesty is a liar). ∴ C(i) false. ∴ C 4th or 5th for Honesty; not 4th, ∴ 5th. ∴ C(ii) false. ∴ higher for Intelligence than for Charm. ∴ not 5th for Intelligence.

2. Consider A(i). If true, then D truthful, ∴ D(i) true, ∴ A a liar. ∴ A(i) not true. ∴ A 4th for Honesty (the only place left for a liar). D not 1st for Honesty. (A(i) false). ∴ D 2nd or 3rd for Honesty. All remarks made by B, D, E are true. ∴ E(i) true, E 3rd for Charm. B or E is 1st for Honesty (no one else can be). From B(i), it cannot be B, ∴ E 1st for Honesty. B not lower than 3rd for Honesty, ∴ from B(i) and (ii) B 1st for Charm, 2nd for Intelligence, 3rd for Honesty. ∴ D 2nd for Honesty (no one else left).

3. A(ii) false, ∴ A higher for Charm than for Intelligence. A not 1st for Charm (B is), ∴ not 1st or 2nd for Intelligence, and not 5th for Charm. From E(ii) total of D's places = 5.

D 2nd for Honesty, ∴ 1st and 2nd for Intelligence and Charm (in that order — B is 1st and 2nd for Charm and Intelligence). Since A not 5th for Charm, ∴ A 4th (no other place left). ∴ C 5th, and since A higher for Charm than for Intelligence, ∴ A 5th for Intelligence.

4. Consider D(ii). We know E higher than C for Honesty and Charm ∴ E lower than C for Intelligence. ∴ C 3rd, E 4th. And complete solution is:

	Honesty	*Intelligence*	*Charm*
1.	Ernie	Duggie	Bert
2.	Duggie	Bert	Duggie
3.	Bert	Charlie	Ernie
4.	Alf	Ernie	Alf
5.	Charlie	Alf	Charlie

75. Cousins and Uncles

From B(1) and B(2) we can draw the following diagram:

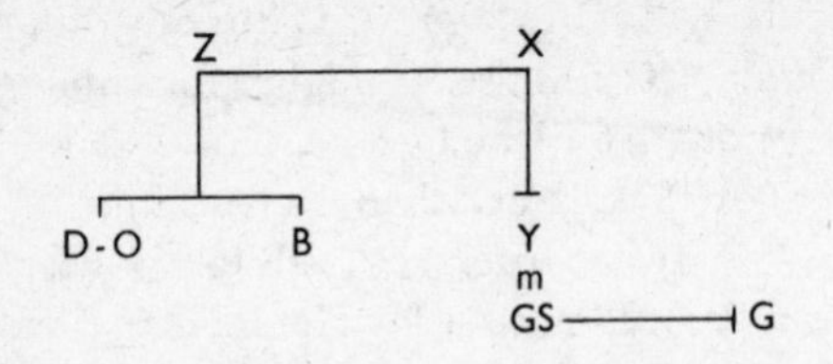

Z is B's father, X is Z's brother, Y is X's son and G's brother-in-law. And GS stands for George's sister. (This diagram accounts for six of the seven people.)

Consider now: G(1): B is D-S's cousin.

D(2): E's son is D-S.

E(2): My father is W.

F(1): My nephew is D-S.

The only combination that will fit these facts and the diagram is for Y to be D-S, for X to be E, for E's father (not represented in diagram, so that he must be the seventh man) to be W, and for Z to be F.

Our diagram now looks thus:

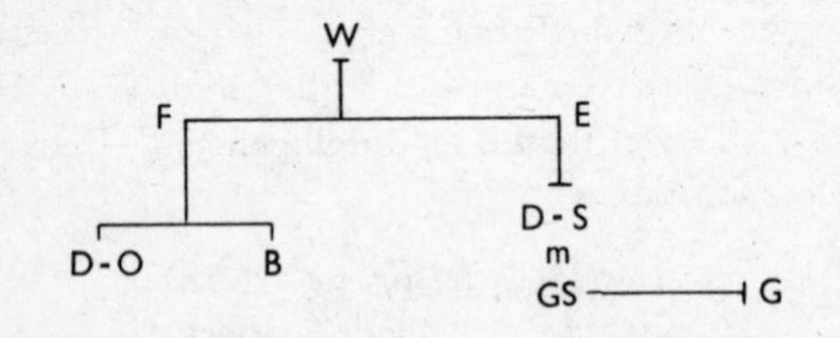

Consider E(1). There are two sets of brothers, E and F, and D-O and B. D and D-K-P cannot be E and F, ∴ D must be D-O and B must be D-K-P.

From D(1): F must be B-W (For F is D's father).

From A(1): A must be D-S, and G must be W-O. (there are no other brothers-in-law).

By elimination, E must be S-U, and C must be W.

Complete solution is therefore: Alf, Door-Shutter; Bert, Door-Knob-Polisher; Charlie, Worker; Duggie, Door-Opener; Ernie, Sweeper-Upper; Fred, Bottle-Washer; George, Welfare Officer.

Charlie is the father of Ernie and Fred. Fred has two sons, Bert and Duggie. Ernie's son, Alf is married to George's sister.

76. Higher Thinking by Alf and Ernie

(i) D is 2 places higher than B. ∴ their places must be 1st and 3rd, 2nd and 4th, or 3rd and 5th.

In order to say what he does A must be able to eliminate two of these. ∴ A must be 3rd. ∴ D must be 2nd, and B 4th.

(ii) E hears this and reaches same conclusion as we have done. As neither A, D nor B is 1st, C must be (E could obviously not have made this remark if he were first).

∴ order is: C, D, A, B, E.

77. Personnel Tests in the Factory

(i) From A's remark and the fact that D was 1st for Ap we can deduce: A not 1st or 2nd for Int; not 1st, 2nd or 3rd for OM; not 5th for Int; not 4th or 5th for Ap.

(ii) C was top or bottom in each test; not top for Ap, (D was) ∴ bottom.

(iii) Here is a table giving possibilities left when we note (i) and (ii) and other facts given:

	Ap	*Int*	*OM*
1.	D	CE	CE
2.	ABE	BDE	BDE
3.	ABE	ABDE	BDE
4.	BE	ABDE	ABDE
5.	C	CE	ACE

(iv) Only C or E can be 1st for Int, and only C or E can be 5th. ∴ C and E between them are 1st and 5th, and E cannot be 2nd, 3rd or 4th.

(v) We must remember that in our table A's places descend from left to right, and B's place is different for each subject.

(vi) With this knowledge, and knowing his own places for Int and OM, D is able to deduce all places except whether C is 1st and E 5th for Int or *vice versa.*

(vii) Investigation will show that there is more than one possibility for D's places which will enable him to do this.

In fact from last piece of information given we see that E must have been 1st for Int (and ∴ C 5th) and D 2nd for Int.

(viii) If D were 3rd or 4th for OM he would not be able to deduce with certainty everyone's place. But if D were 2nd for OM he could reason as follows:

B must be 2nd for Ap (B's places different, he must be 2nd for something). ∴ A 3rd for Ap (no other possibility left), ∴ A 4th for Int and 5th for OM (his places descend from left to right). ∴ B 3rd for Int (no other place left for him). ∴ B 4th for OM (his places all different). ∴ E 3rd for OM and C 1st; and E 4th for Ap.

There is no alternative, and D can reach these conclusions with certainty. But he cannot reach *certain* conclusions if his place for OM is anything other than 2nd.

∴ places are:

	Ap	*Int*	*OM*
1.	D	E	C
2.	B	D	D
3.	A	B	E
4.	E	A	B
5.	C	C	A

78. Intellectual Awareness

Consider A's remark. He is higher than B and his place and B's place must be such that it is possible for C to be 3 places higher than D in one way only; and then of course E's is the remaining place.

The possible positions for A and B so that C is 3 places higher than D are as follows:

(i) 1 & 3 (C 2, D 5).
(ii) 1 & 4 (C 2, D 5).
(iii) 2 & 3 (C 1, D 4).
(iv) 2 & 5 (C 1, D 4).
(v) 3 & 4 (C 2, D 5).
(vi) 3 & 5 (C 1, D 4).

It is therefore certain that A's and B's places must be one of (i) to (vi). But remember that we have no information that C is in fact 3 places higher than D.

E is also able to deduce that A's and B's places are one of (i) to (vi). In addition he knows his own place and assumes (correctly) that B is higher than D. As a result he is able to deduce everyone's place.

Note that 3 comes in four of the possibilities for A and B ((i) to (vi)). No other number comes in more than two of them. If E were 1st (i) and (ii) would be ruled out, also (iv) and (vi) (B is higher than D, ∴ B not 5th), but the following are all possible: E A B C D; E A B D C; E C A B D.

Similarly it can easily be seen that if E were 2nd, 4th or 5th there are at least two possibilities.

But if E were 3rd the only possibilities are (ii) and (iv). (iv) is ruled out because B must be higher than D. E would therefore know with certainty that A and B must be 1st and 4th, and since B must be higher than D he would know that D is 5th, and ∴ C 2nd. These are the only conditions which make it possible for E to arrive, as he does, at the correct conclusion.

The order is therefore: A C E B D.

79. An Intelligence Test in the Factory

Diagrams will help:

1.	A	B	C	D	E
P		×	×		
Q	×		×		
R					
S					
T					

2. *Places*		
1.	BDE, *not* AC	PQRST
2.	ABCDE	PQRST
3.	ABCDE	PQRST
4.	ABCDE	PRST, *not* Q
5.	BDE, *not* AC	PRST, *not* Q

In diagram (1) we can insert information about who is, or who is not, P, Q, R, S, T. In diagram (2) we can insert information, often negative, that, for example, C is not 1st, Q is not 4th, etc.

(i) From P's remark, P not B or C. We cannot tell whether P above both B and C or below them both.

(ii) From Q(1), Q not A or C. If Q(1) false either A or C was 5th, ∴ Q above one of them and therefore above both, ∴ remark true, which is contrary to hypothesis. ∴ Q(1) true. ∴ neither A nor C was 5th, and Q was above A and C. ∴ Q not 3rd, 4th or 5th, and neither A nor C was 1st.

(Information so far has been inserted in diagrams. The reader is recommended to insert further information as it is obtained.)

(iii) From Q(2), Q not E (We cannot yet tell whether Q(2) is true).

(iv) From R's remark, R not C or E.

(v) From S's remark, S not D. If true S would have to be above D, which is impossible. ∴ D not 1st. And S must be below D, ∴ D not 5th, and S not 1st or 2nd.

(vi) From T(1), T not E; from T(2), T not C or A. ∴ by elimination, S is C, P is E, and R is A.

(vii) From diagram (2) we can now see that only B or E can be 1st, and only B or E can be 5th. ∴ B and E between them are 1st and 5th, and they cannot be 2nd, 3rd or 4th.

(viii) ∴ T(1) false, ∴ T below E, ∴ E not 5th, ∴ E 1st and B 5th.

(ix) We know that E is P ∴ P is 1st.

(x) We know that B is 5th and is Q or T, but Q not 5th. ∴ B is T, and T is 5th; and by elimination Q is D.

(xi) Q is not 4th, Q is D, ∴ D not 4th. S is not 2nd, S is C, ∴ C not 2nd.

(xii). Q 1st or 2nd (see (ii)). But P is 1st, ∴ Q is 2nd. ∴ D is 2nd.

(xiii) R's remark is false (E is 1st), ∴ R below C (as well as below E), ∴ R below S (who is C). ∴ R is 4th and S 3rd. ∴ A is 4th and C 3rd.

Solution: 1, Ernie, P; 2, Duggie, Q; 3, Charlie, S; 4, Alf, R; 5, Bert, T.

80. The Birthday Kings

1. C to A. (i). If true, this is false. ∴ it must be false. ∴ C older than A, but not 10 years.

2. C to A. (ii). This is false (see above), ∴ D younger than B.

3. D to B. We know D younger than B. ∴ this is true, ∴ D 9 years older than E.

4. From (2) and (3) we know E younger than B. ∴ E to B true. ∴ E 7 years older than A.

5. C to D. If C 6 years younger than D, then this is true, and C 10 years older than A $(9+7-6)$. But we know this is not true, (see (i)) ∴ C not 6 years younger. If C 6 years older than D this would have to be false, ∴ remark false, ∴ C older than D, but not 6 years.

6. B to C (i). We know this is true, ∴ B younger than C.

7. We now know the order of ages, and some of the differences.

Thus: C, B, D←9 years→E←7 years→A.

8. B to C (ii). True (see (6)) ∴ C 9 years older than D. ∴ B is between 16 $(9+7)$ and 25 $(9+7+9)$ years older than A.

9. Since A to B is true, $\therefore \frac{\text{age of B}}{\text{age of A}} = \frac{170}{100} = \frac{17}{10}$ ∴ age of B is a multiple of 17, age of A is the same multiple of 10; ∴ the difference between their ages is a multiple of 7, and we know it is between 16 and 25, ∴ it is 21. ∴ B is 51, and A is 30.

Rest follows easily.

Ages are: A, 30; B, 51; C, 55; D, 46; E, 37.

81. Holidays Abroad

It is helpful to have a table in which all information, positive or negative, can be inserted as obtained. Thus:

		WIVES					PLACES				
		A	*B*	*C*	*D*	*E*	a	b	c	d	e
MEN	A	×				×	×				
	B		×			×		×			
	C	×	×	×	×	✓			×		
	D				×	×				×	
	E					×					×
PLACES	a	×									
	b		×								
	c			×							
	d				×						
	e					×					

Since of each married couple one member is truthful and the other lies, what anyone says that his or her partner says must be false. ∴ from what Clarissa says Ethel is married to Charlie.

(This information has been inserted in table, together with resultant information that Ethel and Charlie are not married to anyone else. The reader is recommended to insert similar information as it is obtained.)

∴ Charlie and Ethel didn't go to Calais or Ethiopia.

But Daphne said that Charlie went to Ethiopia. ∴ Daphne is a liar. ∴ Beatrice did not go to Dunkirk and Alf is a liar.

And since Alf and Daphne are both liars they are not married to each other. Beatrice said she was not married to Alf. If Beatrice *is* married to Alf she tells the truth (for Alf is a liar), ∴ she couldn't say she was *not* married to Alf if she were. ∴ she is *not* married to Alf and Beatrice tells the truth.

By elimination *Alf is married to Clarissa.*

∴ Alf and Clarissa didn't go to Andorra or Calais. Since Alf is a liar, ∴ Clarissa tells the truth.

∴ *Duggie went to Boulogne.*

∴ Duggie is not married to Beatrice and Daphne did not go to Boulogne.

By elimination *Ernie is married to Beatrice* and therefore they didn't go to Boulogne or Ethiopia.

By elimination *Duggie is married to Agnes*, and since Duggie went to Boulogne ∴ Agnes did too.

By elimination *Bert is married to Daphne*, ∴ they didn't go to Boulogne or Dunkirk.

Since Beatrice tells the truth and is married to Ernie, ∴ Ernie is a liar. ∴ Charlie did not go to Dunkirk.

∴ by elimination *Charlie went to Andorra.*

∴ *Ethel (Charlie's wife) went to Andorra.*

∴ by elimination *Beatrice went to Calais.*

∴ *Ernie went to Calais.*

By elimination *Bert and Daphne went to Ethiopia.*

By elimination *Alf and Clarissa went to Dunkirk.*

Complete solution: Alf and Clarissa went to Dunkirk; Bert and Daphne went to Ethiopia; Charlie and Ethel went to Andorra; Duggie and Agnes went to Boulogne; Ernie and Beatrice went to Calais.

82. Our Factory at Ascot

Diagrams will be helpful.

		WIVES							*WIVES' HATS*						
		A	B	C	D	E	F	G	A	B	C	D	E	F	G
	True or false			×		×									
MEN	A	×			×				×						
	B	×	×	×	✓	×	×	×		×		×			
	C			×	×						×				
	D				×							×			
	E				×	×							×		
	F				×		×							×	
	G			×	×			×							×
WIVES' HATS	A	×													
	B		×		×										
	C			×											
	D				×										
	E					×									
	F						×								
	G							×							

(i) Fill in with ×s, as shown, the information that name, wife's name and wife's hat begin with different letters.

(ii) Consider F(2). Either Flossie or her husband, *but not both,* tells a lie. ∴ Daisy is Bert's wife.

(Fill in this information, as shown, and fact that Daisy is not anyone else's wife, etc.)

(iii) It also follows that Daisy's hat is not B, and that Bert's wife's hat is not D.

(iv) ∴ C(1) false ∴ Clarissa a liar. ∴ her husband not George (C(2)). ∴ C (3) false ∴ Ermyntrude's husband not a liar. ∴ Ermyntrude is a liar.

(All this information has been filled in. The reader may find it helpful to fill in the rest himself.)

(v) ∴ from E(1) Alf is a liar, ∴ Alf not husband of C or E (both liars.)

(vi) From E(2) C's wife wearing an E hat, ∴ C's wife not Ermyntrude, ∴ E hat not being worn by Clarissa (Clarissa cannot be C's wife). Also C's wife not Daisy (she is Bert's wife), ∴ E hat not being worn by Daisy.

(vii) E(3) false. ∴ Clarissa said *Yes*. But Clarissa a liar, ∴ not Ernie's wife.

(viii) B(1) true (see diagram; we know that Alf is not married to Ermyntrude). ∴ all B's remarks true. ∴ B(2) true, ∴ C's husband did say *Yes*. We know that Clarissa is a liar, ∴ her husband tells the truth, ∴ *Fred is married to Gertie*, ∴ Gertie cannot wear F hat, and Gertie cannot wear E hat (worn by Charlie's wife), and Fred's wife does not wear G hat (F's wife is Gertie).

(ix) By elimination *Clarissa married to Duggie*; ∴ Duggie's wife not C hat, and Clarissa not D hat.

(x) By elimination *Ermyntrude married to George*; ∴ George's wife not E hat (already known), and Ermyntrude not G hat.

(xi) *George and Duggie are truthful* (married to Ermyntrude and Clarissa.)

(xii) Consider A(1). We know G *not* wearing an F hat (see (viii)) and we know that George is truthful (xi), ∴ *Agnes truthful.*

(xiii) Consider A(2). We know Agnes and Duggie both truthful, ∴ *Ernie's wife wearing a B hat*, ∴ E's wife not B.

(xiv) Consider D(1). Duggie *is* married to Clarissa. But Alf is a liar, ∴ Alf could not have said it, ∴ *Daisy is a liar*, ∴ Bert (her husband) truthful.

(xv) ∴ D(2) false, ∴ *Ernie is truthful*, ∴ Ernie not married to Agnes (also truthful), ∴ by elimination *Ernie is married to Flossie*, and by elimination *Charlie is married to Agnes*, and by elimination *Alf is married to Beatrice.*

(xvi) Flossie is a liar (married to Ernie, who is truthful (xv)), ∴ F(1) false, ∴ Duggie's wife (Clarissa) not wearing an A hat.

(xvii) Flossie wearing a B hat (see (xiii) and (xv)). We know that Bert is truthful, ∴ G(1) true, ∴ *Gertie truthful.* ∴ Fred lies.

(xviii) ∴ G(2) true, ∴ Bert's wife (Daisy) wearing an A hat.

(xix) D(3) false, ∴ Fred's wife (Gertie) not wearing a C hat. ∴ by elimination *Gertie wearing a D hat.*

(xx) Beatrice married to Alf (liar), ∴ Beatrice truthful. ∴ B(3) true. But Fred a liar, ∴ George's wife (Ermyntrude) not wearing an F hat. ∴ by elimination *Ermyntrude wearing a C hat.*

(xxi) Consider A(3). Agnes truthful, ∴ Clarissa did say *Yes.* But Clarissa lies, ∴ Beatrice not wearing an F hat. (Note that Charlie's wife, A, is wearing an E hat.) ∴ by elimination *Beatrice wearing a G hat*, and *Clarissa wearing an F hat.*

Complete solution:

Alf (liar) married to Beatrice (truthful) who wears a G hat.

Bert (truthful) married to Daisy (liar) who wears an A hat.

Charlie (liar) married to Agnes (truthful) who wears an E hat.

Duggie (truthful) married to Clarissa (liar) who wears an F hat.

Ernie (truthful) married to Flossie (liar) who wears a B hat.

Fred (liar) married to Gertie (truthful) who wears a D hat.

George (truthful) married to Ermyntrude (liar) who wears a C hat.

83. Our Factory on the Cricket Field

It is helpful to have a table, using obvious abbreviations, in which information can be inserted as obtained. Thus:

	×	√ ×	√ ×	√	√
	l-b-b	f-b	o-b	w-k	ump
A					
B					
C					
D					
E					

(√s & ×s represent data about truth-telling)

D(1), (3), (5), are all true or all false (see conditions about truth telling.)

Suppose all true. Then A is w-k (D(5)), ∴ A's remarks all true, ∴ two of opposition were run out (A(3)).

But C and E took 9 wickets between them (D(1) and (3)). This makes 11 wickets altogether, which is impossible. ∴ D(1), (3), (5) are all false. ∴ A not w-k, and since D makes false remarks, D not w-k or ump. ∴ E(1) is true, ∴E(3) is true, ∴E not l-b-b.

A scored 37. ∴ A not ump.

Since E not l-b-b, ∴ A(1) is true, ∴ A(3) is true. ∴ A not l-b-b.

Since, by elimination, A must be either f-b or o-b, ∴ A(2) is false, ∴ C's score is a multiple of 9. ∴ C is not ump.

Suppose B(1) is true; then B(3) is true.

C's score would be a multiple of 63, and D could not have scored 10% more than C (no one scores more than 100, and all scores must obviously be whole numbers). ∴ B(1) and B(3) are false, ∴ B not w-k or ump. ∴ by elimination E is ump, and then, by elimination, C is w-k. ∴ C's statements and E's statements are all true.

From E(2) D not o-b.

Since A(3) is true, bowlers took not more than 8 wickets.

From E(2), D took more than 3 wickets; from C(1) f-b and

l-b-b took same number of wickets; ∴ each took 4 wickets, ∴ from E(4), B scored 32.

B(2) cannot be true, for D would have scored more than 100. ∴ B's remarks all false, ∴ B is l-b-b. ∴ by elimination A is o-b, and D is f-b.

D(2) is true; ∴ C's score less than 32 and a multiple of 9.

D(4) is true; ∴ D's score a perfect square (C(2)), and equal to total of two other scores.

The only possibility is for C's score to be 27, and for D's to be 64 (37 + 27).

∴ final solution: Alf, opening bat, 37 runs; Bert, leg-break bowler, 32 runs, 4 wickets; Charlie, wicket-keeper, 27 runs; Duggie, fast bowler, 64 runs, 4 wickets; Ernie, umpire.

84. Our Factory at Suez

A diagram will help, using obvious abbreviations.

	A	B	C	D	E	F	G	WD	Fr	NBW	PROUN	PE	GDO	WDL
DO														
DS														
WO							×							
DKP														
SU							×							
BW							×							
W							×							
A												×	×	
B													×	
C													×	
D													×	
E													×	
F													×	
G								×	×	×	×	×	√	×

(i) S-U(2) must be true (because no one has a name beginning with a letter after G). ∴ G is GDO. (this fact has been marked in diagram.)

(ii) Similarly any remark about A must be false. ∴ DS(1) is false, ∴ A not PE (mark in).

(iii) WO's remark must be true (we know that GDO is G). ∴ GDO(G) *not* WO, SU, BW or W.

(Mark in, as shown, both that GDO is not these and that G is not these. Other facts are left to the reader to fill in as they are discovered.)

(iv) Since G is GDO who never tells truth about himself, ∴ DO's remark false. ∴ DO not G.

(v) W(1) false (we know W not GDO), ∴ W is not WD, Fr, NBW.

(vi) We know that DS(2) is true, ∴ not made by F or G (who would lie about E) ∴ DS not F or G. ∴ by elimination G is DKP. But G is GDO (see (i)). ∴ GDO is DKP.

(vii) Since DKP is G, ∴ his remarks both false. ∴ B is old BW, and WDL not DO.

(viii) Since B is BW ∴ BW(2) is true. ∴ C is Fr.

(ix) PE not A, ∴ BW(1) made by B about somebody after him in alphabet, ∴ true, ∴ PE is old SU.

(x) SU is PE, ∴ what he says about himself false, ∴ SU not D.

(xi) Since DO's remark false, ∴ DO not WD, Fr, NBW, ∴ by elimination DO is PROUN.

(xii) ∴ by elimination W is WDL.

(xiii) ∴ DS(3) is true, because not made by G. ∴ F is NBW.

(xiv) DO is PROUN, who is not C, F or G, ∴ DO not C, F or G. Similarly PROUN not B.

(xv) WDL is W; WDL not C, F or G. ∴ W not C, F or G.

PE is SU; PE not A, C, F or G, ∴ SU not A, C, F or G. ∴ by elimination WO is F, and by elimination DS is C.

(xvi) F is NBW, and F is WO, ∴ WO is NBW.

C is Fr, C is DS, ∴ DS is Fr, ∴ by elimination BW is WD, but BW is B, ∴ B is WD. By elimination SU is E. But SU is PE ∴ PE is E.

(xvii) W(2) known to be false, ∴ not made by A. Only alternative left for W is D ∴ W is D. ∴ by elimination DO is A. And rest follows easily.

Door-Opener, Alf, PROUN; Door-Shutter, Charlie, Frogman; Welfare Officer, Fred, NBW; Door-Knob-Polisher, George, GDO; Sweeper-Upper, Ernie, PE; Bottle-Washer, Bert, WD; Worker, Duggie, WDL.

85. Names, Names, Names

Diagrams will be helpful. Thus:

	SECOND NAMES				THIRD NAMES				SURNAMES			
	A	B	C	D	A	B	C	D	A	B	C	D
Alf		×	×				×				×	
Bert	×	√	×	×			×				×	
Charlie	×	×	√	×	×	×	√	×	×	×	√	×
Duggie		×	×				×				×	

	THIRD NAMES				SURNAMES					SURNAMES			
	A	B	C	D	A	B	C	D		A	B	C	D
Algernon			×				×		Aaron			×	
Basil			×				×		Balaam			×	
Claude	×	×	√	×	×	×	√	×	Cain	×	×	√	×
Desmond			×				×		David			×	

(i) Suppose Alf (2) true. Then Charlie (1) and (2) both true. ∴ Alf 'imperfect', ∴ Alf (1) and (2) both false. ∴ Alf (2) cannot be true.

(ii) Suppose Alf (1) false. Then Charlie (2) true and Charlie (1) true. ∴ Charlie 'perfect' and Alf 'imperfect'. But this is impossible. If Alf's initial letters are all the same, Charlie's cannot be all different because Charlie would have no name beginning with A. ∴ Alf (1) cannot be false. ∴ Charlie (2) is false, and Charlie (1) is false (since Alf makes one true statement.)

(Mark in diagram, as shown, the fact that Bert is Basil and ∴ is *not* Algernon, Claude or Desmond.)

(iii) Charlie is 'imperfect' (2 false statements), ∴ all names begin with C.

(Mark in diagram, as shown. Other information should be marked in, as discovered.)

(iv) Bert (1) must be false (no one can be 'perfect', see (ii)), and Bert (2) is false (Charlie is Claude); ∴ Bert is 'imperfect' ∴ all his names begin with B.

(v) Duggie (1) is true (see diagram). ∴ Duggie (2) must be false (no one can be 'perfect') ∴ David is Dongle; ∴ by elimination Aaron is Angle.

(vi) Aaron Angle cannot have any other A's (Alf not perfect, no one has 3 A's). ∴ by elimination Duggie is Angle; Desmond is Aaron; Desmond is Angle, and rest follows easily.

Complete solution: Alf Algernon David Dongle, Bert Basil Balaam Bangle, Charlie Claude Cain Congle, Duggie Desmond Aaron Angle.

86. How Old?

Consider first the state of mind of A, and of C who is listening.

For A to have asked (3), the answers to (1) and (2) must have been *No*.

Since A claims to know B's age he must obviously fix it *between* his own age and 51.

Suppose A thinks that B's age is a prime$>51<$his own age, he would then be able to say with certainty that B's age was 53, if he himself was 54, 55, 56, 57, 58 or 59. But in this case C would not be able to deduce A's age correctly. ∴ A cannot think this.

It will be found that the only combination that will enable A to think that he is sure of B's age, and that will also enable C to deduce A's age correctly is for A to think that B's age is not a prime, is less than 51, and greater than his own. If A is 49, he can claim to be sure that B is 50. And when he claims this C can feel sure that A must be 49, for if he were 48 he (A) could not know whether B was 49 or 50.

∴ A is 49 and thinks that B is 50.

∴ the answers that B gives to the questions must be: 1. *No.* 2. *No.* 3. *No.* 4. *Yes.* 5. *No.*

C thinks that B's answers are alternately true and false. But he can't think that (1) and (3) are both false (the number would have to be a multiple of 17 *and* a prime).

∴ C must think that (2) and (4) are false. ∴ C thinks that B's age is: (1) not a multiple of 17; (2) a multiple of 3; (3) not a prime; (4) not greater than 49; (5) less than 51.

C's age is a prime; he knows that B is older than he is; and he claims to be able to deduce B's age.

∴ C must be 47; and must think that B is 48.

We are told that of B's answers two are false; but not (2) or (4) ('although he (C) has guessed correctly how *many* of B's answers are false he has got the wrong ones').

∴ either (1) and (3), or (1) and (5), or (3) and (5) are false. But (1) and (3) cannot both be false.

Suppose D thinks (3) and (5) are false. Then he finds that B's age is: (1) not a multiple of 17; (2) not a multiple of 3; (3) a prime number; (4) greater than 49; (5) not less than 51.

D's age is a multiple of 13, he knows that B is younger than he is, and he is able to announce B's age correctly.

D cannot be 52, for he would then have to think that B's age was a prime number not less than 51 but less than 52, which is impossible.

If D were 65 he couldn't know whether B was 53, 59 or 61.

∴ D cannot think (3) and (5) are false.

∴ D must think (correctly) that (1) and (5) are false.

∴ D thinks that B's age is: (1) a multiple of 17; (2) not a multiple of 3; (3) not a prime number; (4) greater than 49; (5) not less than 51.

D must think that B is 68 or 85. But since he can tell which, D must be between 68 and 85 (and therefore 78, which is the only multiple of 13 between 68 and 85), and B must be 68.

∴ Alf is 49, Bert is 68, Charlie is 47, Duggie is 78.

87. Tom, Dick and Harry

First answer from D cannot be true (if true it is false).

∴ D not *WW*, but D not *P* because he has made a false statement.

∴ D is *SS*, and D(2) true.

∴ T is *P*.

∴ H(2) false. ∴ H(1) false. ∴ H is *WW*.

∴ Tom is a Pukka, Dick is a Shilli-Shalla, Harry is a Wotta-Woppa.

88. Awful, Beastly, Chronic and Dim

(i) D(1) cannot be false, for if it were D would be a *P* and all his statements true.

∴ D(1) true, ∴ D must be a *SS*, and his statements are true, false, true, false.

(ii) ∴ D does owe A 5 rats (D(2) false).

∴ A(4) is true, ∴ A(2) is true (for A must be a *P* or a *SS*).

∴ C is a *P*.

(iii) ∴ B(1) false, ∴ A(3) false (B is not a *P*).

∴ A is a *SS*, and A(1) is false.

(iv) ∴ B(2) is true, ∴ B is a *SS*.

Complete solution: A *SS* (False, true, false, true); B *SS* (False, true, false, true); C *P*; D *SS* (True, false, true, false).

89. Monogamy Comes to the Island

(i) If F(2) true, F must be *SS* (not *WW*, because she has made a true remark; not *P*, because two *P*s cannot be married to each other).

∴ F(1) false, ∴ G is a *P*, ∴ G(1) true, ∴ H(2) false, ∴ H(1) true, (From G(1), H not a *WW*), ∴ F is a *P*. But this is contrary to hypothesis (F must be *SS*). ∴ hypothesis false, ∴ F(2) false. ∴ F *SS* or *WW*, ∴ H(1) false, ∴ H *SS* or *WW*.

(ii) If G(1) true, then H not a *WW*, ∴ H(2) true, ∴ G(1) false, which is contrary to hypothesis. ∴ hypothesis false ∴ G(1) false. ∴ F(1) true (since G makes at least one false remark). ∴ F is a *SS* (F(1) true, F(2) false), ∴ F(3) true, ∴ F's husband is T.

(iii) Since F is *SS*, ∴ T not *SS*. And since F(2) is false, ∴ T not *P*, ∴ T is *WW*.

(iv) G(3) false (because G(1) is), ∴ E not *WW*, and H(3) false (because H(1) is), ∴ E not *SS*, ∴ E is *P* and all E's statements are true.

(v) ∴ S married to G (E(1)), S is *WW* (E(2)), ∴ G not *WW*, ∴ G is *SS* (we know that G(1) and G(3) are false).

(vi) ∴ G(2) true and H(2) false, ∴ H is *WW*.

(vii) Since G(2) true, ∴ U is *P*, ∴ U not married to E, ∴ U married to H, and V married to E.

(viii) Since E(3) is true, ∴ V must be *SS*.

Complete result: Eager (*P*) married to Venal (*SS*); Frolic (*SS*) married to Tired (*WW*); Glorious (*SS*) married to Sordid (*WW*); Happy (*WW*) married to Under (*P*).

90. Discontent in the Island

Denote fathers by their initial letters: P, Q, R, S. Denote mothers by their initial letters: A, E, I, T. Denote sons by their initial letters: w, x, y, z.
A diagram will help:

		WW	*WW*	P				
	A	E	I	T	w	x	y	z
P				×				
Q				×				
R				×				
S	×	×	×	√		×		
w		×						
x	×	√	×	×				
y		×						
z		×						

(i) Suppose I(2) true; then I not *P* (her son is) ∴ I *SS* ∴ I(1) false, ∴ T is *P* ∴ T(1) true ∴ E(2) false ∴ I not *SS* (But this is contrary to our conclusion above that I *is SS* ∴ *our supposition* (*I*(2) *true*) *must be false* ∴ I's son not *P*, and I not *P* (she has made a false statement). ∴ *I's husband is a Pukka.*

(ii) ∴ I(3) false, ∴ I *WW* (I(2) and I(3) both false), ∴ I(1) false, ∴ T is *P*. ∴ T(1) true, ∴ E is *WW*.

(iii) T(2) true, ∴ T married to S (mark in diagram as shown). ∴ S not *P*.

(iv) E(3) false (E *WW*) ∴ x is E's son (mark in diagram as shown). As x is E's son and E is not married to S, ∴ x is not S's son (mark in diagram as shown).

(Reader is advised to insert other facts in diagram as they are discovered).

(v) T(3) true (T is *P*), ∴ E and Q belong to same tribe, ∴ Q is *WW*. ∴ Q not married to E or I. ∴ by elimination Q married to A. ∴ A not *WW*.

(vi) Q married to A, A's son not **x**, ∴ Q's son not **x**.

(vii) A not *WW* (see (v)). A(1) false (see (vi)), ∴ A(1) and A(3) true and A is *SS*.

(viii) ∴ z is R's son, (A (1)) and y is *WW* (A (3)).

(ix) R not married to A or T, ∴ z not son of A or T. ∴ by elimination z is son of I. But we know z is son of R, ∴ R married to I.

(x) ∴ by elimination P married to E, E's son is x, ∴ P's son is x.

(xi) y and Q both *WW*s, ∴ y not son of Q, ∴ by elimination y is son of S. S is married to T, ∴ y is son of T.

(xii) ∴ by elimination w is son of A, and of Q.

We now know the mother and father of every boy.

(xiii) Q, A and w go together; Q is *WW*, A *SS*, ∴ w *P*. T, S and y go together; T is *P*, y is *WW*, ∴ S is *SS*.

(xiv) E(1) false (E *WW*) ∴ x not *P*. But x not *WW* (his mother is) ∴ x is *SS*, and P (x's father) is *P*.

(xv) From I(2) (false), z (I's son) not *P*; and z not *WW* (his mother is) ∴ z is *SS*, and R (z's father) is *P*.

Complete solution: w (*P*) is the son of A (*SS*) and Q (*WW*); x (*SS*) is the son of E (*WW*) and P (*P*); y (*WW*) is the son of T (*P*) and S (*SS*); z (*SS*) is the son of I (*WW*) and R (*P*).

91. All this and Football too

Diagrams will help:

(1)

	P	*WW*	*SS*	*C*	A	B	C	D
P	✓	×	×	✓				
Q	×	✓	×					
R	×	×	✓	×				
S	×				×			
T	×							

(2)

	P	*WW*	*SS*	*C*
A		×		
B				
C				
D				

(3)

	A	B	C	D
A	×			
B		×	2–	
C		–2	×	
D				×

In diagram (1) we can fill in each person's tribe, whether or not he plays for the Cocktail team, and whether he plays for A, B, C or D. (Notice that it is possible for a person to be a *P* (or a *WW* or *SS*) *and* to play for the Cocktail team.)

In diagram (2) we can fill in which team has which letter (A, B, C, D).

In diagram (3) we can fill in the score in each match.

(i) Consider S(1) and S(3). These must either both be true (if S is a *P*), or both false. But if they are both true S is a *WW*, and therefore they are both false. ∴ they cannot both be true; ∴ both false. ∴ A is not the *WW* team; S does not play for A. S not a *P* (he makes false remarks).

(Mark these facts in diagram, as shown.)

(ii) Consider Q(2). If true, T(3) true, ∴ P(2) true, ∴ Q is a *WW*, ∴ Q(2) false. But this is contrary to hypothesis, ∴ Q(2) is false. ∴ Q not a *P*, and T not a *P*. And since Q(2) is false, ∴ Q(4) is false ∴ P is a *P*.

(Notice that this tells us that P is not a *WW* or a *SS*, but it does not tell us that he did not play for the Cocktail team. Also it does not tell us that anyone else is not a *P*.)

(These facts have also been marked in diagram.)

(iii) Since P is a *P*, ∴ P(2) true, ∴ Q is a *WW*, ∴ all Q's statements are false.

(iv) P(1) true, ∴ P. in Cocktail team. P(4) true, ∴ R in *SS* team. P(5) true. Mark in that B scored 2 goals against C.

(These facts have been marked in diagrams. The reader is advised to insert other facts as they are discovered.)

(v) T(3) false (see (iv)), ∴ T(1) false, ∴ D is Cocktail team, ∴ P plays for D.

(vi) Q(3) false (Q a *WW*) ∴ T not a *WW*. But T(1) and T(3) are false ∴ T is a *SS*.

(vii) Q plays for *WW* team (P(2) true), ∴ Q does not play for D.

(viii) Q(1) false, ∴ B not the *WW* team, ∴ by elimination C is *WW* team. And from P(2) since Q plays for *WW* team ∴ Q plays for C.

(ix) R in *SS* team; *SS* team not C or D (*WW* team and Cocktail team), ∴ R not a member of C or D. ∴ R(3) true. ∴ R(1) true (B scored 3 goals altogether). ∴ R not a member of B (see P(3); R's team beat T's team 4–0). ∴ by elimination R a member of A. And since R is in *SS* team, ∴ A is *SS* team. ∴ by elimination B is *P* team.

(x) S not a *P*, ∴ S not in B. T not a *P*, ∴ T not in B. ∴ none of the five are in B.

(xi) T is a *SS*, ∴ T in *SS* team or Cocktail team (A or D). ∴ T not in C.

(xii) P(3) is true. ∴ R's team and T's team not the same. But R's team is A, ∴ T's team is not A. ∴ T's team is D (elimination). S's team is either C or D. But since no team has more than two members, it must be C.

(xiii) From P(3) we now know that A beat D 4–0.

(xiv) S is in C team, C team is *WW*, ∴ S is *WW*. T is in D team, D is Cocktail team, ∴ T is in Cocktail team.

(We have now filled up all the diagrams except (3).)

(xv) R(2) false, ∴ C *v.* D not a draw. T(2) true, ∴ C drew two matches, ∴ C *v.* A and C *v.* B were both draws.

But we know that B scored 2 goals against C (P(5) true). ∴ B *v.* C was 2–2.

(xvi) S(2) false ∴ D did not score more goals *v.* B than *v.* A. But D scored 0 *v.* A, ∴ D scored 0 *v.* B.

(xvii) T(4) true. But D scored 0 *v.* A and 0 *v.* B, ∴ D scored 3 *v.* C.

(xviii) R(4) false. ∴ B did not beat D. But D scored no goals *v.* B. ∴ score was 0–0.

(xix) S(4) false ∴ B won at least one match; not against C or D, ∴ B beat A. From R(1) (true) B scored 3 goals altogether; 2 *v.* C, 0 *v.* D, ∴ 1 *v.* A. And since B beat A, ∴ score was 1–0.

(xx) Q(5) and T(5) are both false. ∴ B's goal average must be equal to C's. We know that B's is $\frac{3}{2}$ ∴ C's must be $\frac{3}{2}$. Let us call score between C and A (a draw) x–x; and score between C and D y–3 (we know that D scored 3 goals against C). Then since C *v.* B was 2–2, ∴ C's goal average $= \frac{x+2+y}{x+2+3}$. Least values of x and y to make this $\frac{3}{2}$ are $x=1, y=6 (\frac{9}{6})$. This makes score between C and D 6–3. And since there is no match in which total of goals reaches double figures, no greater values of x and y are possible. ∴ C *v.* A was 1–1, and C *v.* D was 6–3.

Complete solution: P(*P*) plays for Cocktail (D); Q(*WW*) plays for *WW* (C); R(*SS*) plays for *SS* (A); S(*WW*) plays for *WW* (C); T(*SS*) plays for Cocktail (D); none of them play for *P* (B).

Scores: A *v.* B: 0–1. A *v.* C: 1–1. A *v.* D: 4–0. B *v.* C: 2–2. B *v.* D: 0–0. C *v.* D: 6–3.

92. Clubs and Careers

Diagrams, in which information can be inserted as found, will be helpful, thus:

		CLUBS					PROFESSIONS				
		Booj	ABD	SL	BL	LL	AC	SP	PA	PC	GC
NAMES	A		×					×			
	B			×						×	
	C			×				×			
	D			×				×			
	E										
PROFESSIONS	AC										
	SP										
	PA										
	PC										
	GC										

1. Mark in the information: A not ABD *or* SP; B not SL or PC; D not SL or SP.

2. Consider C's remarks. He cannot himself be SL or SP (mark in). He knows that A is not SP (see (1)). The only person who *can be* both SL and SP is E (see diagram). ∴ C is saying that if he knew E was SL and SP he would know that A was either Booj or LL.

He can only know this if he, C, is BL. ∴ C must be BL (insert this information in diagram). C is also saying that if he knew E was SP, he would know that B was either AC or PA. He can only know this if he, C, is GC. ∴ C must be GC (this and subsequent information should be inserted in diagram as found) and BL must be GC.

3. For E to say that D must be Booj or LL, he must know that D is not ABD. He can only know this if he, E, is ABD himself. ∴ E is ABD. And for E to say that D must be PC or PA, he must know that D is not AC. ∴ E must be AC. ∴ ABD is AC.

4. Mark in also 'additional information': PA not SL; and SP not Booj.

5. By elimination we now have A is SL; B is SP.

6. We know B is SP, and we know B is either Booj or LL, ∴ either Booj *or* LL is SP. But Booj is *not* SP, ∴ LL is SP.

7. By elimination Booj is PA and PC is SL. But A is SL ∴ A is PC, ∴ by elimination D is PA.

8. B is SP, and SP is LL ∴ B is LL; ∴ by elimination D is Booj.

Complete result: A = SL = PC; B = LL = SP; C = BL = GC; D = Booj = PA; E = ABD = AC.

93. The Car of Jones

The answer to each question can be *Yes* or *No*. There are $8(2^3)$ possible combinations for the answers to the three questions. (sq, /sq denote square and *not* square. Other similar abbreviations are obvious.)

The 8 possible answers are:

(i) sq, m19, 5p.
(ii) sq, m19, /5p.
(iii) sq, /m19, 5p.
(iv) sq, /m19, /5p.
(v) /sq, m19 5p.
(vi) /sq, m19, /5p.
(vii) /sq, /m19, 5p.
(viii) /sq, /m19, /5p.

We must now consider which of these combinations can be in Smith's mind. *We must find one which has only one number with a nought in it.* It is not possible for a number to be a square *and* the product of 5 primes. ∴ Smith cannot think the number is (i) or (iii).

(If he thought this he would have 'reason to change his mind about which answers are true and which false'.)

He cannot think the number is (iv) (possibilities: $1024(32^2)$; $1089(33^2)$ and others); nor (v) (possibilities: 3990 $(2 \times 3 \times 5 \times 7 \times 19)$; 6270 $(2 \times 3 \times 5 \times 11 \times 19)$); nor (vi) (possibilities: 190, 380, . . .); nor (vii) (possibilities: 2310 $(2 \times 3 \times 5 \times 7 \times 11)$; 2730 $(2 \times 3 \times 5 \times 7 \times 13)$); nor (viii) (possibilities obviously very numerous).

But if he thinks the number is (ii) (sq, m19, /5p) there is only one which contains a nought; namely 95^2 (9025). ∴ this is what Smith must think.

But he is wrong about the truthfulness of the answers to all his questions. ∴ the number is really /sq/m19, 5p, and it does *not* contain a nought, ∴ 2 and 5 cannot *both* be factors.

If not 2, the least number is $3 \times 5 \times 7 \times 11 \times 13$ (15,015) which is too big. ∴ 2 must be a factor, but not 5.

Least is $2 \times 3 \times 7 \times 11 \times 13$ (6006) but this contains noughts; next is $2 \times 3 \times 7 \times 11 \times 17$ (7854); and next is $2 \times 3 \times 7 \times 13 \times 17$ (9282) which is *too big* (number is less than 9200).

$\therefore$ the number of Jones's car is 7854.

94. Pongle and Quongle play Football

Two diagrams will help — one giving scores in each match as they are found, the other giving information, as found, about the teams to which P, Q, R, etc. belong.

Thus:

	A	B	C	D	E	*Total goals for*	*Total goals against*
A	X						
B		X		*w* 3–1			
C			X				
D		*l* 1–3		X		9	
E					X		

	A	B	C	D	E
P					
Q		×		×	
R					
S		×		×	
T		×		×	

(i) Q, S, T all say, 'score in B *v.* D was 3–1'. If Q, S or T a member of B or D remark false. But Q, S, T cannot *all* be members of B or D. ∴ in at least one case own team not mentioned. ∴ remark true, ∴ neither Q, S nor T a member of B or D. And B beat D 3–1.

(This information has been marked in diagram. Other information should be inserted as found.)

(ii) Q(2) true, since Q not member of D.

(iii) Consider S(2) and T(2) (which say the same thing). S must be A, C or E; and T must be A, C or E. ∴ one of them must be C or E. ∴ S(2) and T(2) false; ∴ C beat E. And S and T between them must be C and E; ∴ no one else is C or E.

(iv) ∴ by elimination Q is A.

(v) ∴ P(1) true (P not a member of either A or C).

(vi) T(3) true (T not a member of B).

(vii) P(2) true (P not a member of C), ∴ C drew against B and D.

(viii) R(1) true (R not a member of C).

(ix) Consider R(2). We know this is false (B *v*. C a draw). ∴ R a member of B or C. But not C (see (viii)), ∴ B.

(x) By elimination P a member of D.

(xi) S(3) true (S not a member of A or B).

(xii) Total against B was 2 goals. Since 1 scored by A, and 1 by D, ∴ none by C or E. ∴ B *v*. C was 0–0.

(xiii) R(3) true, since R not a member of C or D. ∴ score in C *v*. D was 3–3. And since C scored 7 goals altogether, ∴ C scored 4 against E.

(xiv) P(3) true (P not a member of E).

(xv) S(4) false (we know C *v*. D was 3–3).

∴ S a member of C or D. We know not D, ∴ C. ∴ T a member of E.

(xvi) Q(3) true (Q not a member of B or C). ∴ B scored 8 goals. ∴ B *v*. E was 3–0.

(xvii) P(4) true, ∴ A *v*. D was ?–0.

(xviii) Since D scored 9 altogether, ∴ D *v*. E was 5–0.

(xix) T(4) true, ∴ D *v*. A was 0–0.

(xx) R(4) true, ∴ A *v*. E was 1–0.

Therefore membership of teams, results and scores are: P in D, Q in A, R in B, S in C, T in E.

	A	B	C	D	E
A	X	*l* 1–2	*w* 2–0	*d* 0–0	*w* 1–0
B	*w* 2–1	X	*d* 0–0	*w* 3–1	*w* 3–0
C	*l* 0–2	*d* 0–0	X	*d* 3–3	*w* 4–0
D	*d* 0–0	*l* 1–3	*d* 3–3	X	*w* 5–0
E	*l* 0–1	*l* 0–3	*l* 0–4	*l* 0–5	X

95. Frocks for the Frolic

P, Q, R, S, T, stand for the ladies, *l*, *m*, *n*, *o* stand for the materials of the frocks. /*l* means *not* lace, etc.

It will be convenient to put statements, predictions, etc. in shorthand form. (Important to note that from 'If X then Y', we can deduce, 'If /Y then /X,' but we can *not* deduce 'If /X then /Y'.)

Q: If T*l*, then R*o*. If T*m*, then R*m*. Otherwise R*n*.
∴ R/*l* under any conditions. (i)

R: R*l* unless S*m*. But we know R/*l*, ∴ S wears *m*. (ii)

S: If P*l*, then S*o*. But we know S/*o*. ∴ P/*l*. (iii)

P: P*l*, unless R*m* and S/*n*. If (R*m* and S/*n*), then P*o*.
∴ if not (R*m* and S/*n*), then P*l*. (iv)

∴ P*l* or P*o*. But from (iii) we know P/*l*, ∴ P wears *o*. (v)

And, from (iv), since P/*l*, ∴ R*m* and S/*n*. ∴ R wears *m*. (vi)

From Q, we see that the only conditions under which R wears *m* are if T wears *m*, ∴ T wears *m*.

T says, if P/*l*, then Q*l* or Q*m*, whichever is 'worn less by rest of us'. We know P/*l*, and *l* is worn less than *m* by 'rest of us'. ∴ Q wears *l*.

Complete solution: Priscilla, organdie; Queenie, lace; Rachel, muslin; Sybil, muslin; Tess, muslin.

96. The Five Discs

C reasons thus. If anyone were to see two red and two black he would know that he was white. If anyone were to see two red, one black and one white, he would know that he could not be black, for, if he were, the man with the white disc would see two red and two black and would know that he was white. Similarly if anyone were to see one red, two black and one white. If anyone were to see one red, one black and two white, he would know that he could not be black, for, if he were, either of the men wearing white would see one red, two black and one white and would argue as above. If anyone were to see two red and two white he would argue that he could not be black, for if he were, someone would see two red, one black and one white and would argue as above. If anyone were to see one red and three white he would argue that he could not be black for if he were someone would see one red, one black and two white and would argue as above; similarly he would know that he could not be red. Therefore if anyone sees me wearing red or black he can deduce his colour. Therefore I must be white.

(This problem perhaps depends too much on assumptions about the relative intelligence of the people concerned. But some readers may find it an interesting piece of reasoning.)

97. Time Trouble

1. D says time after 11.30 p.m. B (speaking *10 Minutes* later) says *Time* before 10 p.m., and time *30 Minutes* later. ∴ according to B, time is before 10.30. ∴ D and B contradict each other, ∴ not both truthful.

2. C says B and D both liars, and since either everything that C says is true or everything false, ∴ B and D must *both* be liars (they cannot both be truthful). And since C is truthful A is also truthful (see C's last line). ∴ A and C are truthful. B and D are liars.

3. Consider A's (truthful) statement. He says *Time* is *10 Minutes* past some *Hour* (we will call this $x + 10$) and that in *23 Minutes* it will be *75 Minutes* (half of $2\frac{1}{2}$ hours) after *17 Minutes* (half of 34 minutes) before we set off, ∴ it is now *35 Minutes* $(75 - 17 - 23)$ after we set off, ∴ we set off at $(x - 25)$ (G.M.T.)

4. Since we set off *35 Minutes* ago, ∴ time is 35 minutes ahead of *Time*, ∴ time is $(x + 10 + 35)$, i.e. $(x + 45)$.

But B speaks *5 Minutes* after A, and ∴ *40 Minutes* after we started. ∴ B speaks at $(x + 15)$ (G.M.T.). And time when B speaks is 40 minutes ahead of *time*, ∴ time is $(x + 55)$. B says *Time* is before 10. But B is a liar. ∴ x not less than 10.

5. D speaks *10 Minutes* before B (who speaks at $x + 15$ G.M.T.) ∴ D speaks at $(x + 5)$ G.M.T.; and time then is 30 minutes ahead. ∴ time is $(x + 35)$.

D says time after 11.30. But D is a liar. ∴ x not 11. ∴ x must be 10, and since we set off at $(x - 25)$ (G.M.T.), ∴ we set off at 9.35 (G.M.T.).

98. Salamanca Street

(i) (G, H, I, J stand for the people; g, h, i, j for the numbers of their houses).

Consider fact that H's answers to questions are alternately Yes and No.

Answer to 1, 2 cannot be No, Yes ($<g, >i$) for we know that $g<i$; and the answers given are accepted by G and lead to a unique solution, $\therefore$ answers to four questions must be Yes, No, Yes, No. (m3 means 'a multiple of 3', /m3 means 'not a multiple of 3', /sq means 'not a sq'.)

$\therefore$	G thinks:	I thinks:	J thinks:
	1. $>g$	1. $>g$	1. $<g$
	2. $<i$ (49)	2. $>i$ (49)	2. $<i$ (49)
	3. sq.	3. sq.	3. /sq.
	4. /m3	4. /m3	4. m3

From this information G, I and J are able to arrive at unique answers. We now want to find what g must be to make this possible.

I must think 64 whatever g is (the only square between 49 and 99 which is /m3).

For G to arrive at a unique answer, which can only be 25, g must be between 24 and 16 inclusive. But we know that g is odd; $\therefore$ g must be 17, 19, 21 or 23.

J must think answer between 12 and g exclusive, and this answer must be m3 and not a square.

If $g=17$, J thinks 15 (no alternative).

If $g=19$, J thinks 15 or 18.

And if $g=21$ or 23, there are more possibilities. As J arrives at a unique conclusion, $\therefore$ g must be 17, and J thinks h is 15.

(ii) K knows that only two of H's answers are true, and which, and is able to deduce H's number correctly. K must think H's number is in one of these categories:

	I	II	III	IV	V	VI
1.	>17	>17	>17	<17	<17	<17
2.	<49	>49	>49	>49	<49	<49
3.	/sq.	sq.	/sq.	sq.	/sq.	sq.
4.	m3	m3	/m3	/m3	/m3	m3
Possibilities:	many	81	many	impossible	13, 14	none

The only category with a single possibility is II. ∴ H's number must be 81.

Correct numbers: G, 17; H, 81.

Incorrect numbers of H's house: by G, 25; by I, 64; by D, 15.

99. Round the Bend

(i) The possibilities, if the answer 'Yes' is given to questions (1), (2) and (3) respectively are:

(1) 121, 144, 169, 196.

(2) 125.

(3) 116, 145, 174.

Clearly it is not possible for anyone to think that the answer is 'Yes' to more than one question. But in order to say what he does P must think answer is 'Yes' to one of them. It cannot be (2), for P would then claim to know V's number with certainty.

(ii) The possibilities are:

either V has answered 'Yes' to (3), so that if P knows number is greater than 150 he will know it is 174;

or V has answered 'Yes' to (1), P's number is either 169 or 196 and, if he knows number is greater than 150, he will know V's number is the other.

(iii) I knows the questions and answers and has heard P's comment; he also, of course, knows his own number. If V has answered 'Yes' to (3), I will have no information about P's number (except that he has reason to believe that the difference between his number and P's is less than 30) and could not claim to know it. ∴ Answer must have been 'Yes' to (1), and not to (3). And I knows that P must be 169 or 196 (in order to say what he does). And I thinks that V is 121 or 144 (Answer to (1) must have been 'Yes', and I has reason to believe that V is less than 150).

(iv) With this information, his own number, and the belief that the difference between his and P's is less than 30, I claims to know the numbers of both the other houses. He can only do this if his number is 144, and he will then say that V's is 121, and that P's is 169.

∴ I's number is 144 and since I is correct about P's number, ∴ P's number is 169.

(v) Since only V's answer to question (2) was true, ∴ V's

number is not a sq. but is m29; and since I's belief that V's number was less than 150 is incorrect, ∴ V's number must be 174.

∴ numbers are: Proper, 169; Improper, 144; Vulgar, 174.

100. The Island of Indecision

1. Consider B(ii). If true, all E's statements false, ∴ A is a *Q* (E(ii)), and today is Tuesday; ∴ A's statements are true, ∴ B is an *O*, and today is 14th, ∴ B's statements are all false. But this is contrary to our original assumption (B(ii) true), ∴ assumption wrong, ∴ B(ii) false. ∴ E is not *N*.

2. Consider B(iii). If true, date is odd, and in that case all B's remarks would have to be true. But we know that B(ii) is false. ∴ B(iii) false, ∴ B is not *O*. ∴ B(i) false (there are no conditions under which one true remark is followed by two false). Since B(iii) is false, ∴ A(ii) is false.

3. B's remarks all false, ∴ B not *Q* (see conditions), ∴ D(i) true, ∴ D's remarks either all true or alternately true and false, ∴ D(iii) true ∴ C is *P*.

4. ∴ C(i) false (*P*'s only tell truth on Wed. and Fri.). And since *P*'s remarks are either all true or all false, ∴ they are all false, ∴ E is not *P*; B is not *P*. And since *P*'s tell truth on Wed. and Fri. and C's remarks are all false, ∴ today is not Wed., Fri. or Mon. (C(i)).

5. ∴ D(iv) false, ∴ D's remarks alternately true and false. ∴ D is *Q*, and day must be Mon. or Thur. But not Mon., ∴ Thur.

6. ∴ E(i) true, ∴ E(iii) true, ∴ A is *Q*. ∴ E(ii) false, ∴ E is *Q* (since statements are alternately true and false).

7. Since A is *Q*, today is Thursday and A(ii) false, ∴ A(i) true, ∴ date is 14th.

8. B is not *P* (C(iii) false), and not *O* (B(iii) false), and not *Q* (remarks by a *Q* cannot all be false); ∴ by elimination B is *N*. Complete solution: Algernon, *Q*; Basil, *N*; Clarence, *P*; Donald, *Q*; Ernest, *Q*.

The day is Thursday, the 14th.

101. Calculation Crescent

Cuthbert is told two things: (i) that the numbers of 'their 3 houses' add up to twice the number of his house; (ii) that the product of the 3 numbers is 1260.

But this doesn't tell him what the numbers are. ∴ there is more than one possibility.

Some trial of the possible sets of 3 factors of 1260 is necessary here. We want to find different sets whose sum is the same, and this sum must be even (the numbers add up to twice the number of his house).

Remembering that there is no number 1, it will be found that the only two such sets are 4, 9, 35 and 5, 7, 36 (sum 48 in both cases).

These two possibilities must therefore be in Cuthbert's mind when he makes his remark.

Clarence's next remark then tells Cuthbert two things: (i) that the number of his (Clarence's) house is greater than that of anybody else's, (ii) that this information will enable Cuthbert to choose between the two alternatives.

∴ Clarence's number must be 36; the numbers of 'those 3' must be 4, 9, 35; Cuthbert's number must be 24 [$(4+9+35) \div 2$].